THE MARQUIS DE SADE

Selected Letters

THE MARQUIS DE SADE

Selected Letters

PREFACE BY GILBERT LÉLY

TRANSLATED BY W.J. STRACHAN

EDITED & WITH A NEW INTRODUCTION BY
MARGARET CROSLAND

AND WITH AN AFTERWORD BY
JEREMY REED

PETER OWEN • LONDON

PETER OWEN LIMITED
73 Kenway Road London SW5 0RE

First published in Great Britain 1965
This paperback edition, with new Introduction and
an Afterword, first published 1992
© 1963 Société des Editions Jean-Jacques Pauvert
English translation © 1965 Peter Owen
Introduction © Margaret Crosland 1992
Afterword © Jeremy Reed 1992

A catalogue record for this book is
available from the British Library

ISBN 0 – 7206 – 0860 – 0

Printed in Great Britain by Billings of Worcester

Introduction

There was a fashion not too long ago for a kind of superficial literary biography which aimed to link together the Life and Letters of some eminent personality. If the fashion has gone, for many reasons, life and letters in most cases still remain inseparable. The Marquis de Sade wrote many hundreds of letters, some published fairly recently, some unpublished still, some surely awaiting discovery. The group collected here illuminate the life of the extraordinary man who was paradoxically as creative as he was destructive, as intriguing in some ways as he was alarming in others. Most of these letters were written from prison, either the Donjon de Vincennes just outside Paris or the Bastille itself, standing in the heart of the city until it was stormed in 1789. How did it come about that Sade spent over twenty years of his life in custody or detention, and what crimes had he committed?

The man who has bequeathed at least three words to the world – sadist, sadism, sadistic – might have lived a life as comfortable as the eighteenth century would allow. He was born in 1740, son of the Comte de Sade, whose career was spent in the army and the diplomatic service. Marriage had allied him to the younger branch of the Bourbons, while his own family, of Provençal origin, included several lawyers and a great many clerics. Their best-known ancestor was Laure de Sade, none other than Petrarch's Laura, whom the poet first saw in Avignon in 1327. The Comte's son Donatien-Armand-François, the only surviving boy of the current Sade

generation, saw little of his parents and was entrusted to one
of his uncles, an Abbé so worldly as to be immoral, but little
more so than was usual at the time. This uncle acted as his
tutor, while the boy's grandmother and aunts spoiled him.
After a few years at the Jesuit College of Louis-le-Grand in
Paris Sade entered the army at the age of fourteen, rising to
the rank of captain and Maître de Camp, serving in the
Seven Years War (1756–63), learning how to gamble and
how to enjoy the company of young women by paying them
well. He succeeded in doing a great amount of reading but
his senior officers rebuked him for his laziness.

The Sade family had high social standing but no money,
for they were inefficient about collecting the potentially
useful income from their estates, notably the Château de la
Coste in Provence. This made it difficult for the young
Marquis to lead the life he preferred – he wanted
entertainment, in particular he had a passion for the theatre,
he enjoyed paying court to young actresses and falling in love
with them. The old Comte de Sade, described by his son as
'the most affectionate of fathers', paid the young man's
gambling debts, but admitted that his son's 'little heart or
rather body' was 'wildly combustible' and soon realized that
there was only one thing to do: a wife must be found for this
unruly creature of twenty-three, a wife whose dowry would
be useful. Then perhaps the Marquis would settle down.

Of that he had no intention. He fell seriously and
romantically in love with a girl who belonged, as he did, to an
old aristocratic Provençal family. He insisted he would not
accept an arranged marriage, as his family planned, but he
had no choice, especially when his chosen girl preferred
someone else. So in May of 1763 the Marquis de Sade
married Renée-Pélagie de Montreuil.

He married money, which his own family needed, and the
Montreuils, members of the *haute bourgeoisie*, achieved their
ambition, an alliance with the aristocracy. The Marquis's

father-in-law was a Président, a kind of chief justice. He seems to have been a nonentity, dominated by his wife, usually referred to as the Présidente de Montreuil, the woman whose aggressive and vindictive personality was to overshadow the would-be independent Marquis for most of his life. He fought off the marriage as long as he could, still hoping he could persuade his Provençal love, Laure de Lauris, to marry him. Rumours of his conduct reached the Présidente and forced the Comte de Sade to make excuses for his son, saying that he was recovering from a fever and could not return to Paris until he was completely cured. Eventually the Marquis arrived, bringing with him a few dozen artichokes and a tunny-fish pâté. His father had been forced to borrow money in order to outfit his domestic staff for the entertainments occasioned by the wedding ceremonies.

At twenty-three Sade was in no way interested in settling down with a virtuous young wife, however rich, at her family château in Normandy. Like most aristocratic men of the time he rented *une petite maison*, a 'little house', as a means of establishing some irresponsible, enjoyable private sex-life. He found partners easily enough but was not content with straightforward sex, he wanted excitement, and at least one girl complained he had treated her cruelly. He may not have realized that his own family and his in-laws had appointed police inspectors to keep an eye on him, and that through them complaints from the girl were reported to the King. Sade found himself in Vincennes prison but was released after three weeks, thanks to family intervention. His crime was listed as 'excessive debauchery and impiety'.

Despite this inexcusable behaviour Sade was given administrative responsibility the following year when he replaced his father as Lieutenant-General of the provinces Bresse, Bugey, Valromey and Gex. For five years he exchanged his 'excessive debauchery' for the pursuit of the young actresses he had always admired. He was much in love with Mademoiselle Colet but could not afford to keep her. Equally fascinated by Mademoiselle de Beaumont he took her to the Château de la Coste and restored the private theatre there so that they could act together in the plays he had begun to write. He had not deserted his wife: she took part herself in the theatrical performances and seemed to accept everything her husband did. In 1767 their first son, Louis-Marie, was born, a few months after the sudden death of the old Comte de Sade.

Sade was now twenty-seven, virtually middle-aged in eighteenth-century terms, but the next eight years brought his participation in the three 'sadistic' incidents which resulted in his imprisonment. This imprisonment then led to his career as a writer. His attempts to explain his behaviour and defend himself can be read in Letter VII addressed to his wife, 'My Long Letter', as he called it.

He did not, however, tell the whole story. On Easter Sunday, 1768, he noticed a woman who was begging in the Place des Victoires. She was Rose Keller, a 36-year-old widow of German origin, who was looking for work. Sade told her he needed a chambermaid, took her to his *petite maison* at Arcueil and forced her to participate in the classic 'sadistic' scene, beating her with a whip made of knotted cords until he experienced orgasm. He then told her to wash, gave her some eau-de-vie for her wounds, plied her with boiled beef and wine, and locked her in a bedroom. She escaped through the window down a rope of knotted sheets and refused the money offered to her by Sade's valet. Naturally she complained; within three days the local judge was interrogating witnesses and by the fourth day Madame de Montreuil was paying the victim hush-money. Nothing can explain the incident away, while only aristocratic privilege and the Montreuil money prevented serious punishment for Sade. As it was, he was forbidden to live in Paris, was imprisoned for a mere two weeks at Saumur and a further seven months at Pierre Encise near Lyon.

Any other man might have learned his lesson, but Sade was still as 'wildly combustible' as he had been during his army years. Perhaps his ambitious mother-in-law thought he was settling down, especially after the birth of a second son in 1769 and a daughter two years later. But no. In 1772 came the 'affair of the poisoned sweets' in Marseilles, when a group of girls invited to take part in a sexual orgy were given an aphrodisiac, 'Spanish fly', which made them ill. They recovered, but they complained, and Sade's arrest was ordered. He fled to Italy but was condemned to death in his absence. At this juncture Madame de Montreuil was transformed from mother-in-law into a vengeful Fury, for all her plans had gone wrong. Not only had Sade's property been seized by the judicial authorities, he had actually gone to Italy with Anne-Prospère, his wife's sister, who also happened to be her mother's favourite. So much for an alliance with the aristocracy, and who now could be found to marry this younger girl?

The Présidente used all her money and the power it had gained for her. Through various machinations she arranged for Sade to be imprisoned in the Fortress of Miolans in Savoy, at that time part of Sardinia, not France. He escaped and remained in the Château de la Coste, hidden from the authorities. Unfortunately he could not escape from himself, and in My Long Letter (VII) he attempted to explain to his wife how he had come to be in trouble again:

> Seeing myself reduced to passing my time alone in a very remote castle, almost always without your company and suffering from the trifling weakness (I must confess) of being a little too fond of women, I applied to a very well-known procuress in Lyon and said: I want to take three or four servant-girls home with me; I want them young and pretty; supply me with them.

So far he sounded at least honest, if unrepentant, but six months later the parents of the serving-girls wanted their children back. When Sade was accused of abduction and rape he felt he was subjected to 'monstrous injustice'. In the Long Letter he attempts his own defence, but produces only a piece of rhetorical special pleading. He was so bitter about the charges laid against him that he invoked the recent Calas affair of 1762/3, when Voltaire had intervened to redress a miscarriage of justice due to religious intolerance.

For Sade there were to be two more adventurous years: again he fled to Italy, was arrested in Paris on his return and imprisoned at Vincennes. Allowed to appeal against his earlier conviction after the Marseilles affair, he won the appeal, escaped from his escort on the way back to Vincennes, was recaptured and returned to the prison. Indirectly, through more machinations, Madame de Montreuil obtained the support of the authorities and arranged for him to stay behind bars without further trial.

Vincennes, 1777 – 84; Bastille, 1784 – 89; Charenton, officially a hospice for the insane, 1789 – 90; more prison, for political reasons, in 1794, then arrest in 1801 when his so-called obscene books were seized. From 1803 until his death in 1814 he was detained at Charenton, where his family wanted him to remain, out of their way.

His wife, after the long years when she had accepted her husband and everything he did, finally obtained a separation in 1790, but fortunately for Sade he found a new companion, Madame Constance Quesnet, who cared for him and was allowed to live near him at Charenton. He refers to her in Letter XXVIII as 'a charming lady who also has been unhappy and is able to sympathize with others who have had a similar experience'.

This was the background against which Sade wrote his letters: from prison, a few while at liberty and some from Charenton. The letters do not explain his behaviour, or

reveal any truly mitigating circumstances, but they do
explain to some extent the tone of the major novels, *Justine*,
Juliette, *The Hundred and Twenty Days of Sodom*, his need for
revenge on society, the intensity of his iconoclastic anger.
Even if Sade was allowed to write in prison he had to fight to
get the paper and books he needed, even for edible food and
clean clothes.

If Sade wrote at length about sexual cruelty and so far is
remembered for little else, there are occasional references in
his work to the existence of love and even happy marriage.
These letters are the clearest known evocation of his own
marriage and his relationship with his wife. He was almost
totally dependent on her for supplies and help, he needed
everything from ink to biscuits, jam and eye-lotion. When
there was still some faint hope of his release he would implore
her to help him, when there seemed to be no hope left he
would complain about everything she did – he even disap-
proved of the clothes she wore when she came to see him,
after visits had been banned for several years. Why did she
not send him Rousseau's *Confessions*, and why send him
books he could not read twice? When not bitter he could
sound loving, if ironically so. In Letter XIX he loads her with
endearments, beginning with 'Charming creature', pro-
ceeding by way of 'Celestial pussy-cat' and many other
unexpected terms, to 'fresh pork of my thoughts', adding a
footnote: 'I am very fond of pork and eat very little here.'

On one occasion he cannot bear to think she might have
been unfaithful to him, on others he makes indirect
references to their sex-life together: 'you must get a lovely
creature to pose in my bedroom (the sex does not matter; I
have a touch of your family mentality, I don't look too
closely...)'. The 'lovely creature' was to pose 'in the
attitude of the *Farnese Callipyge* – there, presenting it
attractively. I have no dislike of that part; like the Présidente,
I find it more fleshy than the rest, and that, as a result, for

anyone who likes flesh, it is always better than something which is shaved...' (Letter XVII).

Prison made Sade into a writer. He had been something of a writer ever since he wrote love poems as a young man, as most educated people did, but rancour, loneliness and shortage of money turned him into a professional. As a result he never forgave his wife when she apparently neglected to remove the manuscripts remaining in his room at the Bastille after it was stormed. He felt that years of his life had been stolen from him twice over.

Gilbert Lély, who discovered and edited these letters, dwells in his Preface on Sade as a precursor of the Surrealists and as someone gifted for black humour, long before the term was invented. No authentic portrait of the Marquis has survived, as far as is known, but his true if controversial image can be found in these letters. Some passages can be linked to the ideas expressed in the books, notably for instance Sade's belief that punishment was useless, or his attacks on the iniquitous judicial system prevailing under the *ancien régime*. Like prisoners of all types and in all ages Sade found it necessary to invent endless means of passing the time or making confinement tolerable. Even for him writing was not enough, it could not occupy every moment of the day. He began to play curious games with numbers, working out what Gilbert Lély calls 'a system of deduction based on calculations which appear ridiculous to us, but which to his way of thinking were likely to reveal the date, for which he desperately hoped, of his release'. He would seize on any number, such as the number of lines in a letter, or the number of times a word was repeated, and interpret this as a 'signal', an announcement that could somehow lead to a calculation of the longed-for day. If it was impossible for these 'signals' to carry any clear indication of future events, Sade simply became fascinated by the figures for their own sake. Sometimes he would confuse the issue by introducing word-play, as in Letter XVII. It is worthwhile remembering that while he was including this kind of private mathematical game in his personal letters, he was working out the seemingly impossible permutations and combinations of human sexual behaviour in the fantasies of the major books.

During the eighteenth century in France, as in other countries, writers both professional and amateur wrote endless letters, often using the epistolary form to compose a novel. Sade himself employed this technique in his novel *Aline et Valcour* of 1795. Most of his own letters are not literary, despite the classical allusions, the mentions of books and authors, and the pages here and there of would-be close reasoning. His letters are *un cri écrit*, to use Cocteau's phrase, a written cry for help. Whether he deserved such help is another matter. In the meantime he offers his readers, as he always did, many surprises: he tells his wife of a moving dream about Laure de Sade, how she invited him to join her in heaven. He tells his lawyer about the time when he had acquired administrative power during the period of Revolutionary Terror: 'I had the Montreuils put on a recommendations for mercy list. I had only to say the word and they would have had a rough time. I said nothing; that's how I take my revenge!' Paradoxically, the man who had spent his life in advocating atheism seems to have remembered, late in life, the Christian message of forgiveness. It is a message that the readers of these letters might do well to contemplate.

Margaret Crosland
1992

NOTE

The material which forms the basis of this Introduction and of my notes to the translated text which follows is based principally on the invaluable pioneering research in France of Maurice Heine and Gilbert Lély. Some obscure references must unavoidably remain unexplained. (M.C.)

Preface to the Letters

In January, 1948, I had the good fortune to discover, at the Château of Condé-en-Brie, home of the direct descendant[1] of the Marquis de Sade, a priceless collection of letters which was to reveal a new, or at least barely known aspect of the literary genius of the author of *Justine*. This collection consists of one hundred and seventy-nine letters, with additional lists of requests, notes and registers which bring the total number of documents to about two hundred and fifty. The collection may be classified as follows:

(a) Forty-two letters written from Vincennes Prison, between February 1777 and June 1778.

(b) One hundred and twenty letters also written from the same prison from September 1778 to February 1784, after a period of liberty limited to a few weeks.

(c) Seventeen letters written from the Bastille between February 1784 and September 1785.

Three-quarters of this correspondence is addressed to the Marquise de Sade. The other recipients are, in order of quantity of documents: the Présidente de Montreuil,[2] Marie-Dorothée de Rousset,[3] Le Noir, Lieutenant-General of Police, the valet Carteron, alias La Jeunesse, alias Martin Quiros, the lawyer Gaufridy,[4] the Abbé Amblet,[5] the police officer Martin, the Commandant de Rougemont, the oculist Grandjean and the young Donatien-Claude-Armand de Sade, the Marquis's eldest son.

1 Notes on the text appear at the end of each section.

I have edited eighty-one of these one hundred and seventy-nine letters and published them in three anthology collections entitled : *L'Aigle, Mademoiselle. . . . Le Carillon de Vincennes, Monsieur le 6*, the last one in collaboration with Monsieur George Daumas.

The vast majority of de Sade's letters are not dated, or else give only the day of the month or sometimes only the day, but a detailed checking system usually makes it possible to attribute a fairly precise date to them. As a rule, they are written on a piece of card folded in half and covered on both sides with very close lines. The handwriting is always exquisitely elegant. The longest letters consist of sixteen pages, while some of them consist only of two. They have no margins and according to their size, which varies between $3\frac{3}{4}'' \times 4\frac{3}{4}''$ and $7\frac{1}{4}'' \times 10''$, they contain from two hundred and fifty to six hundred words to a page. De Sade obviously wrote them without making a draft, in moods of despair, indignation or tragic gaiety. Only very few passages are crossed out, and often nothing is crossed out at all. Four or five letters stand out from the others in a poignant fashion through the size and clumsiness of the handwriting.[6] (They belong in fact to one of the periods when the Marquis was suffering acutely from the eye trouble which first attacked him in February, 1783.)

In addition to this correspondence there is an unpublished collection of thirty or so letters addressed by Madame de Sade to the prisoner in Vincennes.

Nearly all the de Sade letters published before my collections, notably those – easily the most numerous – which appear in the *Correspondence* edited by Paul Bourdin, belong to the period dating from the time de Sade left Charenton,[7] on 2nd April 1790, to the result of the decree by the Constituant Assembly relating to prisoners detained under a *lettre de cachet*, and his incarceration in Sainte-Pélagie,[8] 5th April 1801, by the police of the First Consul. His twelve years of captivity at Vincennes and in the Bastille (1777–1789) were only represented by four

letters in Paul Bourdin's collection, and by the letter of 4th
October 1779 to Martin Quiros, published by Maurice Heine.
Now the correspondence discovered at the Château of Condé-
en-Brie relates precisely to the first part of these twelve years,
merciless years in de Sade's existence, when his enemies 'buried
him alive', in the prime of life when his erotic imagination was
nourished by intoxicating experiences – deep within first one
and then the other of the two most sinister sepulchral fortresses
in the kingdom.

The letters published by Paul Bourdin are vitally interesting,
because they reveal de Sade's behaviour during the Revolution
and because some of them have a high literary value. I have
included eight of them in the present collection. Most of the
letters however are addressed to his lawyer, Gaufridy, which
means that requests for money and problems concerning the
management of his possessions predominate. On the other hand,
in spite of his indulgence for the companion of his youthful
pastimes, de Sade rarely found himself in the mood to confide
to him his most intimate thoughts; he soon discovered that
Gaufridy had acted as secret agent to the Présidente de Montreuil since 1775, and had continued to do so up to the outbreak
of the Revolution.

The letters from the Marquis which I have published are
written in a very different vein and are nearly all addressed to
the only person whose profound attachment, and even heroic
devotion, de Sade had been able to appreciate in many circumstances, namely, his wife. His sarcastic remarks and fits of
rage concerning the slightest contrariness on her part – reactions
easily excusable in his atrocious seclusion – must not mislead
us about Madame de Sade's conduct nor about the Marquis's
true feelings for her. In spite of his reproaches and his ever-
active distrust – perhaps he hoped by arousing her *amour-
propre* to make her more energetic, for in his agony of waiting
he considered her too slow-moving or ineffective – he must have
been aware that his wife's entire existence was taken up with

attempts to obtain his liberty, that in order to win such an achievement Madame de Sade shrank at nothing and put forward the most touching pleas to the Ministries every day. Therefore, as far as he could hope that his letters might escape police censorship or the indiscretions of the Présidente de Montreuil, he had no hesitation in confiding to the Marquise many of his most secret desires, since he could have no fear that the person who had given him so many proofs of love could take action against him.

I have seen the prison of Vincennes, a gigantic tomb with four flanking towers, and climbed the spiral staircase which led to his place of torture. I was filled with pity by the sight of the cells : narrow, disproportionately high and condemned to the eternal twilight filtering through one loop-hole window with a double row of bars. It was in one of these ice-cold cylinders, in this atmosphere of funereal horror, that the Marquis de Sade wrote his letters, fine examples of eloquence and imagination with which only the most universal products of the Elizabethan genius can be compared.

What fills us with admiration when we read the Marquis's letters for the first time – once he has passed through the acute despair of the first months of captivity – is their constant and lofty lesson in strength of mind, combining the integral maintenance of ideas which earned for their writer the torture of seclusion and the expression of a supreme form of humour which certainly constitutes the most heroic and most effective human defence against the aggressions of external reality.

The Marquis de Sade never seeks to refute the general opinion of his character any more than he does his morality and his metaphysics, however dangerous such obstinacy must inevitably have been to his hopes of liberation. 'Imperious, angry, hot-headed, extreme in everything, imaginative about morality in a way more disorderly than the world has ever known, atheist to the point of fanaticism, in fact, that is what

I am like, and once again, kill me or take me as I am, for I shall not change'.[9] Out of the twenty other statements of the same kind to be found in the letters from the incoercible prisoner, I will quote only the following : 'My way of thinking is the outcome of my reflections; it results from my existence, my constitution. I am powerless to change it; if I could, I would not. The way of thinking that you criticize is the one consolation of my life; it lightens all my sufferings in prison, it provides all my pleasure and I cling to it more than to life itself. It is not my way of thinking that has caused my misfortune, it is that of others'.[10]

I have alluded earlier to the vital part played by humour in the unpublished letters of the Marquis de Sade. I shall now develop this point further.

I have always believed that from an aesthetic point of view tears are finer than laughter, a preference already justified by Lautréamont in *Les Chants de Maldoror* (IV) : 'Oh, execrable degradation ! We look like goats when we laugh !' Sometimes however laughter can be as fine as tears, and this is when, in the form of transcendant humour, it constitutes, as I said earlier, a manifestation of human heroism. 'Humour,' states Freud, quoted by André Breton[11], 'has not only a quality of release . . . but there is also . . . something sublime and lofty about it. . . . The invulnerability of the ego asserts itself triumphantly. The ego refuses to let itself be damaged, to let external realities impose suffering on it, it refuses to admit that the traumatic experiences of the outside world can touch it; what is much more important, it demonstrates that they can even become opportunities for pleasure'.[12]

De Sade's brilliant revolt while in prison gives remarkable proof of such a definition and does not fail to correspond to the most modern aspects of that 'black humour' of which André Breton's anthology includes many examples. The names which occur to us when we first read the Marquis's letters are those of Lautréamont, Jarry and Nietzsche. We know that one

of Lautréamont's most important inventions consisted of inter-
polating, in the midst of a piece of writing, disjointed phrases
taken from works on medicine or the natural sciences. We can
find in de Sade's letters (XIX of the present volume, for
example) the same uprooting process which was to become one
of the key features of Surrealism. In letter XXIV comes the
disconcerting appearance, for 1784, of the female Ubu, the
Présidente Cordier, complete with her 'sublime reasoning'. The
dialogue form at the beginning of the letter, as well as the
presence of a foil, in this case the governor of the Bastille, adds
to a resemblance which does honour simultaneously to the
Marquis de Sade and Alfred Jarry.[13]

The Marquis's correspondence includes many passages and
even entire letters which, though not corresponding precisely
to the contemporary definition of 'black humour' (although the
fact that de Sade has the courage to write them during his
terrible seclusion would suggest such humour), nevertheless
belong to a superior form of comedy, similar also to lyricism,
and comparable too, with certain passages from Aristophanes
and Shakespeare. To show how this form of humour differs
from the low manisfestations of laughter considered as an end
in itself, it could best be described as 'solar' and I will add a
general observation likely to illuminate de Sade's great erotic
novels : his letters reveal the aspect of transcendant mystification which is contained in *La Nouvelle Justine* and *Juliette,* but
without being at all incompatible with the combination of
lyricism and descriptive psychology of these books.

Of all the years during which the Marquis wrote letters,
1783 produced the most outstanding examples, notably the
letter of 23rd and 24th November (XIX in this volume); it
could be described by the phrase used in a very different sense
by the valet Carteron who wrote one day to his master : 'It
looks as though a swarm of bees have been feeding on your
paper'. The erotic boldness of its opening, the tone of exquisite

lightheartedness which distinguishes it, the finesse and firmness of its language, and its continuously enchanting grace can make such a letter comparable to the music of Mozart, who knows so well how to make us aware of human dignity. Moreover, the Marquis de Sade reveals himself once more as a precursor of the modern sexologists and at the same time seems to defend his future enterprise : 'I respect tastes, fantasies : however odd they may be, I find them all worthy of respect, because we are not in control of them, and because the strangest and most bizarre of all, when carefully analysed, is always due to a *principle of refinement*'. This identical viewpoint was upheld a century later by Havelock Ellis when he wrote that the phenomena of erotic symbolism, which show us the individual stripped of everything, 'presuppose a very highly developed plastic power of the imagination (and) constitute the supreme triumph of human idealism'. De Sade, in 1783, explicitly formulated the content of such a thought, which can be considered as the philosophical peak of Havelock Ellis's work : 'You know that nobody analyses things as much as I do'.

The discovery of the Marquis's correspondence, with its important new revelations, is perhaps comparable – in a different field – to the discovery, early this century, of the scroll-MS of *The Hundred and Twenty Days of Sodom*.[14] The great novels by de Sade which were published during his lifetime have earned for him, from the language point of view, a fame which very few French writers deserve to share. But in spite of the erotic boldness of their vocabulary, in spite of the unparalleled inversion they describe, *La Nouvelle Justine* and *Juliette* still seem to observe a certain number of conventions inherent in the 18th-century novelist's art, and which even a mind as original as de Sade's could not contemplate abandoning entirely. No preoccupation with taste or composition and no literary ulterior motive ever arise in his correspondence, and he did not believe that it would one day be published. Nobody, before the Romantics, wrote with such total freedom, except possibly the Duc de Saint-Simon. And despite their sincerity and stylistic perfection, how timid and cold seem Rousseau's *Confessions* compared with de Sade's letters! Incredibly, the Marquis's correspondence foreshadows, by a whole century, the subjectivity successfully expressed in the work of the Comte de Lautréamont, Arthur Rimbaud and Alfred Jarry.

The uneasiness with which many people still approach de Sade's major works, such as *The Hundred and Twenty Days of Sodom, Justine* and *Juliette,* prevents them from fully appreciating the many elements contained in them. The unpublished correspondence, first made public a few years ago, from which I have selected the finest passages, will justify the secret admiration which these readers feel, still with some anxiety, for his works. From now on they will find release through the essentially human presence of these letters and the poignant diversity of their tone which arises from an immediate tragedy. They will be able to consider the Marquis de Sade as an 'admissible' genius, like Shakespeare, Pascal or Nietzsche; they will be able to enjoy his dark erotic paradise without guilt, either by regarding his books as descriptive psychopathology or by studying them from the point of view of language and the dialectic of opposites with which that other pessimistic *grand seigneur,* the Comte de Lautréamont, has long been credited.

The three collections of letters written at Vincennes will, I am sure, place the Marquis de Sade once more among the greatest writers of poetic realism, in spite of the hostile attacks launched against him at every period of history.

GILBERT LÉLY

NOTES

1 The Marquis Xavier de Sade.

2 De Sade's formidable mother-in-law. See Introduction. (*Ed.*)

3 Mr Geoffrey Gorer has given such an intriguing description of this lady, a friend of the Marquise de Sade, that I cannot hope to better it: 'an indefatigable, sprightly, provincial blue-stocking, well-meaning, muddle-headed and consumptive, incurably arch and daring in her conversation and letters'. The Marquise de Sade was upset by the flirtatious letters which passed between her husband and Mademoiselle de Rousset, but unnecessarily so. (*Ed.*)

4 Referred to variously as 'notary' and 'agent', he came from Apt in Provence and acted on de Sade's behalf for several years. Madame de Montreuil craftily began to bribe him and he accepted money from her while giving her in return useful information about her son-in-law's doings. De Sade partly suspected this but had no proof. (*Ed.*)

5 De Sade's former tutor. (*Ed.*)

6 For example, Letters 36, 37 and 38 in *Monsieur le 6*.

7 A refuge for the mentally deranged, run by the Frères de la Charité. De Sade was sent there for nine months, on this occasion, after behaving somewhat strangely while in the Bastille. Amongst other things he would go to the cell window and shout to passers-by that the prisoners were being murdered and everyone must come to their help. (*Ed.*)

8 A former convent which, during the Revolution, became a prison for political offenders. De Sade was sent there in 1801 to be punished 'administratively' as the author of *Justine* and *Juliette*. (*Ed.*)

9 Letter XX.

10 Letter XVIII.

11 In his *Anthologie de l'humour noir*, Paris, Editions du Sagittaire, 1940 (published only in 1945).

12 It is hardly necessary to mention here that the 'pleasure' referred to by Freud has no connection with enjoyment of a masochistic kind.

13 Letter XXIV.

14 This extraordinary work was written in microscopic handwriting on a long roll of paper consisting of five-inch wide
sheets stuck together to a total length of about thirteen yards.
The MS was found in his room after his departure from the
Bastille and nothing more was heard of it until 1904 when it
was published by Ivan Bloch in Berlin. It had been bought by
a German collector from the French family of Villeneuve-
Trans, who had kept it for three generations. (*Ed.*)

LETTER I

To Madame la Présidente de Montreuil

(Vincennes, end of February 1777)

Of all the possible courses that vengeance and cruelty could choose, you must admit, Madame, that you have taken the most horrible of all. The moment I came to Paris to hear my mother's last dying whispers and with no other purpose than to see and embrace her for the last time, or mourn her if she had ceased to live, that precise moment would have to be the one you chose to make me your victim once more. Alas, in my first letter I asked you whether it was a second mother or a tyrant that I was to look for in you, but you have not left me long in doubt! Was it in this spirit, tell me, that I wiped away your tears when you yourself had lost a father whom you worshipped? And on that occasion did you not find my heart as sensible to your grief as to my own? It was not as if I had come up to Paris in defiance of you or with any plan in mind which might have caused you to desire my removal! . . . But next to the attention which my mother needed, my aim was merely to move you, to come to a mutual understanding with you and take all the decisions in the present affair which you would have agreed to and indeed advised. Independently of my letters, Amblet,[1] if he is honest (which I doubt) should have already told you all this. But my treacherous friend and you have plotted to deceive and ruin me; not without a measure of success. When they brought me here they told me that it was to settle my case, and that because of this, my

B   35

detention here was necessary. But, in the name of all that's honest, how can I be fooled by such talk? And when you used the same means in Savoy² did you achieve anything at all? Have my two absences – each of a year's duration – had the slightest effect? And is it not patently clear that it is my utter ruin that you desire and not my rehabilitation?

I would like to share your belief for a moment that a *lettre de cachet* is indispensable to avoid a lawsuit which is always disagreeable, but need it have been so severe, so cruel? Would not a letter banishing me from the kingdom have achieved the same object? And would I not have surrendered myself with the same rigorous correctness, since I had just put myself in your hands of my own free will, ready to submit to whatever you demanded? When I wrote to you from Bordeaux asking for money to enable me to cross into Spain and you refused, it was further proof that it was not my exile from this country that you sought, but my imprisonment; and as I reflect on the circumstances, everything leads me to suppose that you never had any other intention. But I am mistaken, Madame : Amblet has revealed another and one that I mean to carry out. He told me, Madame, no doubt on your behalf, that a *death-certificate* was the one indispensable document calculated to bring this wretched affair to a swift conclusion. You must obtain this, Madame, and I assure you that you will not have long to wait. As I shall not write more letters than necessary, as much on account of the difficulty of writing them as of their failure to move you, the present one will sum up – rest assured of this – my final feelings. My plight is terrible. As you are aware, neither my constitution nor my mind could ever stand close confinement. Even under much less rigorous detention – as you will well know – I have risked my life to gain my freedom. Means to do this are denied me here, but one way out is left, a way which surely no one will deny me and which I intend to use. My mother calls out to me from the depths of her tomb : I seem to see her open her bosom once more to clasp me to it – the only refuge I have left. It is a comfort to me that I shall follow so closely, and my last wish, Madame, is that you should have me laid beside her. Only one thing restrains me; it is, I admit, a weakness on my part. I should have liked to see my children. It used to be such a sweet solace to go and embrace them after I had seen you. My new misfortunes have not banished a desire which I shall probably carry with me to my grave. I commend them to you, Madame. At least cherish them even if you hated their father. Give them an education which will preserve them, if that be possible, from the disasters into which neglect of my own has dragged me.[3] If they knew my wretched lot, their souls, modelled on that of their affectionate mother would throw them at your knees, and they would raise their innocent hands to try and move you. It is my love for them that evokes this comforting picture, but it will achieve nothing, and I hasten to destroy it lest it bring too much emotion to bear on moments when my sole need is for resolution. Adieu, Madame.

NOTES

1 The Abbé Amblet, de Sade's former tutor.

2 A reference to de Sade's arrest at Chambéry through Madame de Montreuil's influence with the King of Sardinia. (*Ed.*)

3 Ironically, in one sense, this is what happened. De Sade's elder son turned against him to such an extent that he even took unpublished MSS to the police after his father's death and asked for them to be destroyed.

LETTER II

To Madame de Sade

(Vincennes, 6th March 1777)

Oh! my dearest one, when will there be an end to my horrible plight? When, in the name of Heaven, are they going to release me from the tomb in which they have buried me alive? Nothing could equal the horror of my fate! no words can describe my sufferings nor convey the anxiety which torments me, nor my all-consuming grief! All I have here are my tears and my cries; but no one hears them. . . . Where are the days when my dearest wife shared them? Today I have no one; the whole of nature seems dead to me! Who knows whether you even receive my letters? The absence of any reply to the last one I wrote proves beyond doubt that they do not hand you them and that I am allowed to write to you only as a means of easing my distress or giving away my thoughts. The latest refinement, inspired doubtless by the fury of the woman who is persecuting me! What does so much cruelty portend? Try and imagine the kind of state my poor head must be in. Hitherto a faint hope has sustained me, comforted the first moments of my terrible distress: but everything conspires to destroy it, and from the silence in which I am abandoned and the state in which I find myself I can see clearly that all they want is my downfall. Would they set about it thus if it was done for my good? They surely realize that the severity with which they treat me can only result in sending me mad and that consequently the sole outcome (supposing they wanted to save my health) can be to

38

do me a great injury. For I am convinced that I cannot stand a month here without going mad : that is no doubt what they intend and it fits in wonderfully well with the methods they contemplated this winter. Ah! my dear wife, I see my fate only too well! Remember what I told you more than once, that they wanted to let me finish my five years in peace, and then. . . . It is this idea that is torturing and slowly killing me. If it lies in your power to relieve me on that score, please do, I implore you, for my present state is terrible and you would sympathize, of that I am sure, if you could really appreciate what it is like. Nor have I any doubt that they are trying to drive a wedge between us; that would be the final blow which I assure you, I should not survive. I entreat you to oppose this attempt to divide us with all your might and realize that our children would be the first victims; there is no case of children being happy when there is disharmony between their father and mother. My dear wife you are all that I have left on this earth : father, mother, sister, wife, friend, you represent all of them, I have only you; do not abandon me, I beg you, let it not be from you that I receive fate's final blow.

Is it possible – if they intend any good purpose – that they do not realize that they are ruining everything by this punishment? Do they imagine that the public will probe more deeply into the matter? People will merely say, '*He must have been guilty since he has been punished.*' When a crime is proved, such means are used either to appease a Parlement[1] or prevent it from pronouncing sentence; but when it is certain that there is no crime and that the sentence has been the height of madness and malice, punishment should not be administered, for then all the good that might have been achieved by annulling the sentence is undone and they demonstrate beyond all doubt that it has been solely a matter of favour, that there was an offence and that the king had been asked to punish it to avoid the Parlement doing so. Now, I claim that this is the worst thing they could do to me, it means ruining me for the rest of my life;

some years ago your mother found out that public opinion never changes in such cases and always eyes with disfavour anyone who has made himself liable to punishment by the king or the Parlement. But that's what she's like : when something has to be done, she puts herself in someone else's hands and is deceived, with the result that I'm done much more harm than she had often intended. It's the story of Saint Vincent, tell her that I beg her to remember that; there is somebody else here who is up to the same game and it is not difficult to guess who that person is.

Finally, my dear wife, all I ask you as a favour is to get me out of here as soon as possible, at whatever cost, for I cannot bear it any longer. They tell you I am very well; you find comfort in such news; good, I am very glad. I will not undeceive you since I am forbidden to. That is all I can say. But remember this – I have never endured a situation like the one I am in today and that in the circumstances in which I found myself,[2] it is a scandal that your mother should have landed me in it. The wretched lawyer who said that it was inhuman to pile woe upon woe little knew your mother when he said it. Until the happy day which releases me from the horrible torments in which I am plunged, I entreat you to obtain permission to come and see me, to write to me more often than you do, to persuade them to let me take a little exercise after my meals which, as you know, means more to me than life itself, and to send me my second pair of sheets without delay. I haven't shut my eyes for the last seven nights and have been vomiting at night all the food I have eaten during the day. Get me out of this place, my dear wife, get me out, I beg you, for I feel that I am dying by inches. I cannot understand how they could have been so callous as to refuse me my camp-bed; such a slight favour, but it would have at least allowed me to forget my misfortunes for a few hours each night. At any rate, send me my sheets forthwith, I do entreat you. Adieu, my dear wife, love me in proportion to my sufferings, I ask no more, and believe me, I am in the depths of despair.

NOTES

1 From the fourteenth century onwards courts of justice were set up in many large French provincial towns because the Parlement, or high court in Paris (which lasted until 1791) could not deal with cases from all over the country. De Sade refers here to the Parlement of Aix which had sentenced him to death in his absence, in 1775. See Introduction. (*Ed.*)

2 On his arrival in Paris, de Sade had just learnt of his mother's death three weeks before.

LETTER III

To Madame de Sade

(Vincennes, 18th April 1777)

They are quite right, my dear wife, when they say that the houses one builds in my present plight are built only on sand, and that all the plans one makes are mere fantasies no sooner conceived than destroyed. Of half-a-dozen schemes which I had thought out and on which I was founding my hope for an early release, not a single one, thank God, remains. Your letter of 14th April dispelled them as the rays of the sun dissipate the morning dew. It is true that, on the other hand, I found consolation in the sentence '*I could be quite sure that I would not be kept here a minute longer than is necessary.*' I can think of nothing more reassuring than this expression, so that if they think it necessary for me to remain here six months, six months I shall remain. It is charming, and truly, those who guide your behaviour have every reason to congratulate themselves on the progress you are making in their profound art of poisoning the wounds of hapless victims. You could hardly be more successful. I warn you however that my mind cannot hold out any longer against the cruel life I endure. This is clear to me, and I prophesy that they will have good ground for repenting for having subjected me to severity so unwarranted and so unsuited to my temperament. It is, they claim, for my own good. A divine phrase in which one recognizes the usual jargon of *triumphant imbecility*. It is for a man's good to expose him to the risk of going mad, for his good that you destroy his health, for his

42

good that you feed him on the tears of despair! I confess that up to now I have not been happy enough to understand and appreciate this 'good'. . . . You are wrong, the fools tell you gravely: *it makes a man think*. It is true, it does; but do you know the only thought this infamous brutality has engendered in me? The thought, deeply engraved in my mind, of fleeing as soon as I can a country where a citizen's services in no way compensate for a momentary aberration, where imprudence is punished as if it were a crime, where a woman, because she can scheme and cheat, discovers the secret of enslaving innocence to her caprices, or rather finds it in her powerful and individual interest to bury the real source of the whole affair – of fleeing the land and far from trouble-makers and their accomplices seeking out a country where I may by serving faithfully the Prince who offers me asylum, deserve at his hands what I could not obtain in my own country . . . justice and peace.

Such, my dear wife, are my sole and unique reflexions, and I aspire only for the happy moment to put them into effect. We have, you say, been induced into error. Spare your breath. . . . I assure you that I was not deceived for one minute, and you cannot fail to remember that a moment before your room was filled with *a band of ruffians* – who without producing any order from the King, came nevertheless, they said, to arrest me in the King's name – I told you to put no faith in that reassuring letter from your mother, and that since she displayed some human feeling, you could be sure that her soul was feeding on deceit. No, my dear wife, no, I might be surprised, but I shall never be deceived when I set eyes on this frank and worthy creature – which is unlikely to be very soon. In coming here, I have followed the example of Caesar who said *'that it was better to expose oneself once in one's life to the dangers one feared than live in the perpetual anxiety of avoiding them'*. It was this philosophy that took him to the Senate where he knew that the conspirators awaited him. I have acted similarly and like him I shall always be greater through my innocence and frankness than my enemies by their baseness and the secret rancours that actuate them. You ask me how I am. But what use will it serve for me to tell you? If I do, my letter will never reach your hands. However, I am going to satisfy you, since I cannot imagine that they would be so unjust as to prevent my replying to what you are permitted to ask me. I am in a tower, locked behind nineteen iron doors, receiving daylight by two small windows, each provided with about a score of iron bars. For about ten or twelve minutes of the day I have the company of a man who brings me my food. I spend the rest of my time alone and in tears. . . . That is my life. That is how a man is corrected in this country – by breaking every link with society with which he should be reconciled so that he may be led back to the path from which he has had the misfortune to stray. Instead of good counsel and advice I have my tears and despair. Yes, my dear wife, that is my lot. How do you expect them not to cherish virtue when it is offered under such divine colours! With regard to the way I am treated, there is doubtless some element of decency in it . . . but mixed with it are so many petty deprivations and puerilities that when I arrived I felt as if I had been transported to the island of the Lilliputians where men, being only eight inches high, behave in a manner befitting their stature. At first it made me laugh, since I could not get it into my head that people who seemed reasonable were capable of such stupidities. Then I became exasperated. In the end I try to imagine that I am only twelve years old – a more charitable course than if I pretended that *they* were that age – and this idea of being thrown back into childhood slightly alleviated the distress that a reasonable man would otherwise feel to see himself treated thus. But one altogether touching thing that I almost forgot to tell you is the eagerness with which they appropriate you here, down to the smallest play of your facial expression which they straightway report to the relevant authority. At first I was taken in, and my

heart, whose moods are dictated solely by your letters, let out
an indiscretion one day when I had received a note from you
that had delighted me. How promptly the notes which followed
it brought home my stupidity! From that moment I resolved
to be as two-faced as the rest of them, and at the present time
I am composing my features in such a way as to challenge the
shrewdest of them to read my feelings from my facial expression. Oh well! my heart, there you see at any rate one virtue
acquired! I defy you now to come and tell me that one gains
nothing from being in prison! Concerning the walking and
exercise you advise me to take, you talk in truth as if I were
in a country house where I could do what I liked. . . . When
they let the dog out it goes and spends *one hour* in a kind of
cemetery about forty square feet surrounded by walls more
than fifty feet high, and this charming favour is not granted
as often as one would like. You realize – or at least you should
now realize – how many inconveniences would result from
allowing him the freedom one allows to animals : he would only
have to become well suddenly and what the devil would happen
to all the projects of those whose sole aim is to make the man
die? For the sixty-five days that I have been here, I breathed
the air for about five hours on five separate occasions. Compare it with the exercise you know I am accustomed to take,
which is absolutely necessary to me, and you can judge of my
state! The result is terrible headaches which refuse to leave
me, dreadful nerve pains, vapours and a total lack of sleep –
all of which may sooner or later bring on a serious illness. But
what does it matter provided that Madame Présidente is satisfied and that her clod of a husband can say : 'That's good, that's
good, this will make him think!' Adieu, my heart, keep well,
and love me a little : it is only this thought that can soothe all
my troubles.

Nothing has been brought for me to sign. It was hardly
worthwhile announcing this request to me so much in advance
only to see nothing come. And then the extract from it you

give me is merely intended to vouchsafe me a glimpse of the most tedious passages. I am therefore going to ask permission to name an attorney to act on my behalf. First, you will have to gain the said permission, then name the attorney, explain the position to him and induce him to act. . . . Note the delays and the vast amount of time! Add to all that the correct way in which they urge me to sign the papers and you will see that it will require an eternity. It is true that what consoles me is *that I shall not remain here a minute longer than is necessary!*

Adieu, once more, my dear good wife. You have here a long letter which will probably never reach you since it is not written on the Lilliputian model. Never mind, at any rate it will be seen, and who knows whether of all those who are to see it you are the one to whom I address it most directly?

I am delighted to hear the things you tell me about your children. You cannot conceive of the joy with which I shall embrace them, although I cannot delude myself – despite my affection – so far as not to realize that it is for their sake that I am undergoing my present ordeal.

As I read this letter through it becomes clear that it will never reach you – a solid proof of the injustice and horror of all the sufferings they inflict upon me, for if there was nothing but what is just and simple in all that I feel, why should they fear to tell you or let you know? However that may be, I will not write to you again until I have definitely received a reply to this, for what is the use of writing if you do not receive my letters?

LETTER IV

To Madame de Sade

(Vincennes, 17th February 1779)

I am replying to you with my usual exactness, my dear wife, for there is nothing easier for you than to count my letters and see if there are any missing: you have only to count your own.

I am not incapable of writing to you, truly, and if I were, rather than cause you anxiety since I know how you feel towards me, I would be so clever, that you would not notice it. But tell me, I beg you, what you mean when you keep repeating: *'If you cannot write to me, get someone else to write for you'*? Doubtless you imagine that I have secretaries at my command: alas, think how far I am from having such a luxury when I scarcely have my most essential needs! A man – always in a great hurry – appears in my room four times a day, including once at dawn to enquire *whether I have slept well* (you see how far their attentions extend), the other occasions to bring me my food etc. Seven full minutes is the exact amount of time he spends with me altogether during these four visits; and then there's an end of it: *'Die if you wish of grief and boredom; it's all one to us.'* – Tell me please if one can be said to have secretaries when one is reduced to that! But perhaps you will object 'you didn't tell me that before.' And in truth they looked after me much better before; formerly I was allowed to go for walks much more often; they never left me to myself when I was eating; I was in a good room where I could

47

make a good fire. . . . And now, no one when I eat; many fewer walks; and, cramped in the dampest room in the dungeon (and it is this that brings on my headaches). And to crown my delight no possibility of making a fire here; for such as you see me, I haven't lit it all through the winter, and I can assure you also that I shall not be lighting it either. That is how it is with me, my dear wife. But furthermore, I am now no longer needed : my case has been judged. If I die, so much the better; good riddance. . . . And I am utterly convinced that nobody will really care. And you don't insist that in such a situation that I should most urgently beg to be let out, or at least be told how long I am to remain here? I should have to be very much my own enemy not to be preoccupied with this single thought, as preoccupied as both those who keep me here and those who refuse to satisfy me concerning the sole consolation that I ask for, are with me. . . . You are not aware of it, you say ! And if you are not aware of it, how do you come to pass it on to me? Do not repeat such a lie, in the name of God, do not repeat it, for it makes my blood boil. I will prove to you in the most unambiguous way that you knew by the 14th February 1777 that I was to be tried on the 14th June 1778. Now, if you knew so much about this first period of my detention, how do you hope to convince me that you did not know about the second? But what am I saying? . . . Alas! You do not refuse to tell me, and you do indeed tell me in as forceful and expressive a way as you have indicated to me the sixteen months with your number 22.[1] Is there anything clearer than the *Saturday 22nd February, No. 3 finally*? To doubt, after that, that my day of release is not 22nd February 1780 would be indeed to cherish a very hopeless illusion. But, in case I should not be sufficiently convinced, you were good enough to send me three papers to sign very shortly afterwards assuring me that it was for 'three years'.[2] By renewing this charming indication today, precisely today with two years gone by and one more to come, you urgently demand another signed document ! And after indications of

this kind you expect me to have further doubts? No, no, no, I
do not doubt for a minute that I have another wretched year
to suffer. It is useless for you to insist on that point any longer,
I understand, I comprehend, do not bring up again this fear-
ful reminder. The shameful thing about it, the thing I will
never forgive the men and women who are responsible, is the
fact that they are trying to rid me of this idea instead of con-
firming it. When at the beginning you brought home to me this
idea of three years so emphatically, why now that I repeated
it here, did they reply : 'What a notion! three years, it's impossible! a few months at the most. . . .' That is the infamous part
of it, the most odious feature which has contributed so much
grief and wretchedness to my situation. Would it not have been
infinitely more human to leave me to my illusion, since it was
not a fancy, than to destroy it each day and permit me to form
a hope which they fostered, nay excited in me, solely to savour
the misery in which the mortification of seeing it destroyed was
to put me? I repeat, such methods are odious; they are as much
lacking in humanity as they are in common sense; they bear
only the stamp of a brutish ferocity like that of lions and tigers.
And now when more inured than ever to this very real idea
that I have still a year to suffer, as my letters testify – always
harping on the same theme, they have the audacity to write to
me concerning twelve pots of preserve which I am requesting
in the month of December : *twelve pots of preserve! great
heavens! what do you expect to do with that? Doubtless you
are giving a ball? In any event it will not greatly matter if there
is some left.*' That is the kind of thing that has been and is the
work of my executioners, for how else can one name those from
whom I have received the most vicious stabs in the back? Once
you mentioned *three years*', once I expected it, why destroy
my illusion? Why allow me to catch a glimpse of an earlier
release when it wasn't true? And why, finally, have the kindness to offer me hope at every moment, only to snatch it away
the next? It is of this infamous game that I am complaining,

and those who are playing it are acting as instruments of vengeance for other people and fulfilling a very mean, and wicked role, nay, barbarous, for what have I done to these people? To one of them nothing : I had never set eyes on him in my life; the other I had overwhelmed with kindness and civility. . . . Well, everything is now said; they can sharpen their knives for next year, if perchance my illusion is too favourable; because, as for the latter, I now declare to them that accustomed to their odious lies they may say and write until kingdom come but I will not expect to leave here a minute earlier than 22nd February 1780. Let us say no more about it. One sentence from your letter, however, conjures up the possibility of an even more dreadful fate. It is this : *'nothing proves that the terms I have indicated to you according to my own conjectures are false.'* But the terms to which you refer are limited to the date, 22nd February 1780. I declare and protest that I have neither seen nor guessed any other hint in your letters. Yet, in the next sentence you write : *'Your reply to that will be "but why did you indicate this or that at La Coste?" My reply will be that I was tricked.'* But what you indicated at La Coste was that they had told you that I would still be here three years after my sentence, or else one year followed by exile. At the present time you say you are annoyed for having sent me that information. That makes it even worse, for surely one is not annoyed for having told someone *more* than there is : it would be preparing a nice surprise for him; one does not make anyone an apology for having deceived him in that way. . . . However, you make me one. So that it is worse; and if it *is* worse, I am a long way out in my reckoning if I think I shall leave this place on 22nd February 1780! I would be greatly obliged for an explanation of the phrase, for it is causing me a great deal of cruel anxiety and distress.

Tell me, I beg you, do you ever ask the infamous rogues, the horrible beggars who divert themselves by keeping me on tenterhooks by withholding the date of my release, what they

hope to gain thereby? I have already said and written hundreds
of times that instead of winning they are losing the battle;
instead of doing me good they are doing me the most grievous
harm, and that my character is not of a kind to be treated in
such a way, that they are taking from me both the possibility
and the will to meditate on my conduct and consequently profit
by the opportunity I am afforded. Furthermore I certify today,
after two years of this horrible situation, that I feel a thousand
times worse than I did when I arrived, that my temper has
grown bitter and obstinate, my blood boils a hundred times more
easily, my head is a hundred times worse, and that, in a word
–when I leave here, I shall have to go and live in a wood, so
impossible will it be for me in my present state to live among
human beings. And what, after all, would it cost me to say
that this treatment does me good if it had in fact done so? Alas,
Messieurs Apothecaries, now that your drugs are paid for and
two-thirds consumed, why should I not agree as to their efficacy
if they had any? But, believe me, they have none, save that of
inducing madness, and you are poisoners, not doctors, or rather
villains who deserve to be broken on the wheel to teach you to
keep an innocent man locked up for the sole satisfaction of
your cupidity and your nasty, petty personal interests. And
should I keep quiet about it? May I be utterly annihilated if I
do! 'Other people have been their victims,' you will say, 'and
have not said a word about it. . . .' They are animals, imbeciles;
if they had spoken, unveiled all the horrors, all the infamies of
which they have been the victims, the monarch would have
heard about it; he is just and would not have allowed it; and
it is precisely their silence that these blackguards exploit. But
I will reveal the truth, I will open people's eyes, even if I have
to throw myself at the King's feet and demand redress and
justice for all the wrongful sufferings I have had to undergo.

Oh! You do not need to recommend me not to work out my
calculations[3] from, or refer to, your letters! I give you my word
of honour that I no longer do so. I have done it for my sins, for

I thought I should go mad, but I would rather be tortured with red-hot irons than do it again. You turn a deaf ear to No. 22. . . . The question I asked you was very simple, but you are unable to satisfy me; let's say no more about it. Just remember that I will never forget your cruelty. . . . Well, if you had a good memory, you would recall whether all those strictures on my character were successful. The difference that there was between me at La Coste, after the diverting scandals they had just instigated and myself when I was left in peace. . . . You should be able to see after that whether all this is doing me any good. I wish to allude only to what you yourself told me about it. If Milli[4] Rousset cannot tell what she does not know, let her say nothing; that is my sole reply; she must listen to me. If she sulks, so much the worse for her; she shows how much trust you can put in your friends in this present age, etc.

May one enquire who has married Milli Devri? Milli de Launay[5], you say, is not married, *and I shall not go to her wedding.* She must surely be going to get married since you are preparing not to attend her wedding? Consequently, Marais[6] did not lie to me so much as you make out. But, what he did lie about was when he told me that I would not be here more than six weeks. That's where I consider him an abominable wretch because he knew all the time that it was not true and it was shameful to say less than the truth for it is preparing the most desperate moment for a man when he sees his hope frustrated. – I am not signing the paper. It is a signal. It has had its effect; let us say no more about it. Have you not got the money from Provence? Send for it if you need it; but I am signing nothing.

My only comfort here is Petrarch. I read him with a pleasure and avidity which is indescribable. But I treat it the way Madame de Sévigné treated her daughter's letters: *I read it slowly for fear of having read it.* How well this work is composed! . . . Laura turns my head; I am like a child about her; I read her all day long and at night I dream of her. Listen to a dream I had of her yesterday while the whole universe was amusing itself.

It was about midnight. I had just fallen asleep with her Memoirs in my hand. Suddenly she appeared to me. . . . I saw her! The horror of the tomb had not impaired the brilliance of her charms, and her eyes had the same fire as when Petrarch celebrated them. She was draped in black crêpe and her beautiful blonde hair floated carelessly above it. It was as if love, to preserve her beauty, was anxious to soften the lugubrious effect of the mourning in which she appeared before my eyes. 'Why do you moan on earth?' she said to me. 'Come and join me. No more ills, no more sorrows, no more trouble in the vast spaces that I inhabit. Have the courage to follow me there.' At these words I flung myself at her feet and said, 'O mother! . . .' And my voice was choked with tears. She proffered a hand which I covered with my tears; she too shed tears. 'When I lived in this world which you hate,' she added, 'I used to enjoy looking into the future; I extended my posterity as far as you yourself but never saw you so wretched.' Then absorbed in my tenderness and despair, I threw my arms about her neck to hold her back or follow her and water her with my tears, but the ghost had disappeared. All that remained was my grief.

> O voi che travagliate, ecco il cammino
> Venite a me se'l passo altri non serra.
> Petrarch' Sonnet LIX

Good night, my dear wife, I love you and embrace you with all my heart. Have a little pity on me, I beg you, for I assure you that I am more wretched than you imagine. Judge of all my sufferings; and the state of my soul shares all the darkness of my imagination. I even send my love to those who cold-shoulder me since it is only their injustices that I hate.

This 17th February, after two years in these terrible chains.

NOTES

1 An example of the 'signals' which de Sade regarded as clues to the date of his release. See Introduction. (*Ed.*)

2 In 1777 the Présidente de Montreuil had forced de Sade to sign three documents by which she received, in his place, the revenue for three years from his office as Lieutenant General on behalf of the King in the provinces of Bresse, Bugey, Valromey and Gex.

3 A further reference to de Sade's obsession with numbers. (*Trans.*)

4 'Milli' is a diminutive of 'mademoiselle'.

5 De Sade's sister-in-law and his mistress in 1772.

6 Inspector of Police.

7 De Sade was a descendant of Petrarch's Laura. See Introduction. (*Trans.*)

LETTER V

To Martin Quiros[1]

(Vincennes, 4th October 1779)

Martin Quiros . . . you are being an impudent fellow and if I were there, I would give you a thrashing. . . . I would snatch off your blasted false *toupet* which you renew every year with hairs plucked from nags' tails on the Courtheson-Paris road. And how would you set about repairing it, you old roué? You'd go off like a Picardy peasant beating down nuts – snatching right and left at all those black objects that hang outside the shops in the evenings along the rue Saint-Honoré, then, next day, with the help of a touch of glue you would fix them on your scurfy forehead so skilfully that it wouldn't be any more obvious than a crablouse on a whore's c. Isn't that the truth, my man? . . . For God's sake keep your mouth shut for a bit; I've had enough of this endless stream of insults from the rabble. It's true that when I see this great pack of curs and bitches barking at me, I act like a dog and lift up my leg and piss on their noses.

F—— me; there you are as learned as an encyclopaedia! Where did you collect up all those delectable items? . . . stuff about elephants killing Caesar, Brutus stealing oxen, about Hercules,[2] the Battle of Sheep's eyes, and that Varius affair! Oh, it's all very amazing. I expect you filched the information one night on your way back from taking your mistress out to have supper with her at her old nurse's; you stuffed all those items into the back of her dress as you went along, and then

55

you imitated the man who dropped his cherry stones there, so that the poor marchioness arrived back in the evening with elephants, Hercules's and oxen in her dress and she had to sit up as stiff as a ramrod, as if she hadn't been a *Présidente's* daughter. Although you talk to me about a pregnant woman, it wasn't for pregnant women that I gave you my recipe, I gave it for you . . . are you with child, or is Madame Patulos? Or else is it Mille PRINTEMPS? tell me . . . tell me who it is who is pregnant among you? Upon my word I don't care who it is, you remember my ditty: *'Luckily I don't care a b——'* well, I sing it six times a day and whistle it four.

What you old b—— of an ape, you squitch-face smeared with blackberry juice, vine-prop of Noah's vine-yard, backbone of Jonah's whale, old whorehouse fire-lighter . . . rancid candle at twenty-four *sous* a pound, rotted saddle-girth of my wife's moke . . . so you've not found any islands for me; you dare tell me that, you and your four friends of the frigate awash, rolling round the entrance to the port of Marseilles, you've not been to find any islands for me; you've not found seven for me in a morning? Ah: you ancient pumpkin cooked in bugs' juice, third horn of the devil's head, codface, drawn out like the two ears of an oyster, slipper of a procuress, Milli Printemps's blood-stained petticoats – if I had you here I'd rub your nose within it, your dirty baked potato snout that looks like a burnt horse-chestnut – to teach you to lie like this.

How you come it over me because you're not seasick; what do you expect me to say to that, my lad? I've known for long enough that you can carry your *wine* and your water better than me but while you swagger about on deck, it would only need a pasteboard serpent to make you jump into the sea or Hell itself if it gaped at your feet . . . every one of us has his weak-nesses my lad Quiros . . . lucky the man who has the fewest. But what's all this talk about Venice? I've never been to Venice; it's the only town in Italy that I don't know but I'll be going there one day, I hope. As for coxswain Raviol, it's a

different matter. I know him; I've had the distinction of being
his captain for three weeks, and I recall that we attacked the
Bridge at Arles together, at which battle I lost a great number
of men and I was obliged to retire with dishonour and without
having taken part in any boarding. During the said time, you
who cannot swim like me and who for that reason do not like
naval battles, went along the river bank with your saddle
on your head like a tortoise and with your top-boats in your
hands as if they were gloves trying to join forces with a Monsieur Rétif.[3] Ah; I have not forgotten your deeds of derring-do !

I was very pleased to hear that my squadron was in the
roads. I will not delay joining it, with my skiff the *Fracasseur*
I am merely waiting for sixty or eighty pieces of cannon and
forty iron trusses which are at the foundry and which I want
to hoist up to the main-top to make it look more formidable
and then I'll set sail to cruise about this spring.

You say then, my son Martin, that my writing is not to your
taste; just listen to my reasoning on this subject.

I write only for my wife who reads my writing very well
however bad it may be. Those who with no qualification or any
right whatsoever insist on poking their noses into this writing
which does not please you can go and f—— themselves. If
you want the verdict of scholarship on the point now, well here
it is my son, and the male and female who give themselves these
airs, far from getting angry about the place to which I con-
sign them, will give me the reply, if they are anxious to avow
openly their tastes in this matter, that the schoolmaster made to
a woman who complained to him that Cardinal Dubois had
sent her where I am sending them. 'Madame, the Cardinal is
insolent. But sometimes he gives good advice.' Farewell Quiros.
My compliments to Gautruche when you see him; tell him that
I am delighted about his resurrection and above all I beg you
not to forget to remember me to Milli PRINTEMPS.

This 4th in the evening on receipt of your third letter or on
the dot as Milli Printemps says.

NOTES

1 Carteron, nicknamed Martin Quiros, or La Jeunesse, the valet and copyist of the Marquis.

2 De Sade is assuming that his valet has picked up lots of miscellaneous classical information à la Sganarelle and has mixed it all together in his uncomprehending brain. (*Trans.*)

3 Rétif de la Bretonne, the writer, whom de Sade disliked.

LETTER VI

To Monsieur Carteron (Martin Quiros)

(Vincennes, beginning of January 1780)

I eagerly snatch this opportunity, Monsieur Quiros, at the start of a new year to wish you and all you care about the compliments of the season. In short, my woes and misfortunes are diminishing, Monsieur Quiros, and thanks to the great protection of Madame La Présidente de Montreuil, I hope, Monsieur Quiros, to be able to express my compliments in the flesh the day after tomorrow five years hence. Long live influence, Monsieur Quiros! If my fatal star had linked my destiny with some other family, I might be in for life, for you must know, Monsieur Quiros, that in France you cannot with impunity fail in respect towards prostitutes. You may speak ill of the government, the King, religion; that's nothing. But a whore, Monsieur Quiros, great heavens! A whore, you must be careful not to offend her, for immediately your Sartines[1], Maupéous,[2], Montreuils and other mainstays of the brothel will in the *best martial manner* rally in support of the whore and *intrepidly* lock up a nobleman for twelve or fifteen years for the sake of a whore. So there is nothing finer than the *French Police*. If you have a sister, niece, or daughter, Monsieur Quiros, advise her to become a whore; I defy her to find a worthier profession. And in fact where can a girl be better off than in a State where, in the lap of luxury and ease and in a continual state of drunken debauchery she can still find so much backing, as much credit, as much protection as the most respectable *bourgeoise*? That is what is called encouraging manners, my friend;

59

that is what is called turning respectable girls against filth. God, how heartfelt it is! Oh, Monsieur Quiros how intelligent we are in our century! As for me, I give you my word of honour, Monsieur Quiros, if heaven had not seen fit to place me in a condition to provide my daughter[3] with bread, I swear to you by all that I hold most sacred in this world, I would instantly set her up as a whore.

I hope, Monsieur Quiros, that you will allow me to offer you for your New Year gift a new little work, chosen by the *messenger boys* of your dear mistress and very worthy of their taste. To be sure, I thought the reading of this little work might interest you and I am parting with it for your sake. It is anonymous; great authors, as you know, trying to appear under a cloak. But as we book-lovers like to pierce the mask, I think I have discovered who the present author is, and if it is not by the ruffian at your street corner, it must certainly be by Albaret. This worthy offspring could have been fathered only by one or other of these two great men : *the market-hall or the magistrature* – there's no half-way house. The close resemblance of these two touches is the cause of my error : it is so easy to ascribe to one pen what comes from the other, and it's wonderfully easy to make a mistake. It's like the pictures of Carraccio and Guido – those two illustrious masters rise to the sublime so equally that one sometimes confuses their brush strokes ! God Almighty ! Monsieur Quiros, it's a pleasure to talk to you. The Palmieri, the Albinis, Solimenas, Domenicos, Bramantes, Guercinos, the Michelangelos, the Berninis, the Titians, the Paul Veroneses, Lanfrancos, Espagnolets, Luc Giardinos, the Calabri etc., you are as familiar with all these people as Sartine is with prostitutes and Albaret with procurers. But when I want to talk about these matters here, they've no idea what I mean. There's only one man, *Lieutenant Charles*[4], a very well-informed person who will tell you whenever you like that in *the twelfth century* the dungeon of his fortress was besieged *under cannon fire*. But one has not the luck to chat with him as often

as one would like . . . he is like *Molé*,[5] he only performs on
Fête days.

I have enriched the enclosed book with some notes which
will serve to explain the text and I hope you will find them of
interest, Monsieur Quiros. And I flatter myself that you will
keep this small present from me all your life. I have sent along
with it a somewhat old-fashioned and somewhat salacious song
but I trust it will amuse you and your friends all the same,
Monsieur Quiros, when you come and eat a stew or rabbit with
bacon at Vincennes, La Rapée or La Redoute.[6]

By the way, Monsieur Quiros, do me the kindness to inform
me whether you are in fashion and whether you have runners'
shoes, harness buckles and a windmill on your head. I have a
special desire to see you dressed in that style, and you must
be very interesting in that get-up. The other day I wanted to
crown my head with one of the said 'windmills'. It belonged
to monsieur le lieutenant Charles who was *'playing'* that day
(it was fine); well, Monsieur Quiros, how like a cuckold it made
me look once my head was crowned with that felt affair. Oh!
where did the air come from, Monsieur Quiros (because there
was some)? Was it in the hat? Was it on my brow? Was it inside Monsieur le lieutenant Charles? It is a question that I
leave to you to decide.

I would be sincerely obliged to you if, out of gratitude for
my attention to you, you would be kind enough to send me a
small paper model of your friend Monsieur Albaret's *headpiece.*
I have a pregnant woman's fancy to see a specimen of the said
gem. Take down his hatter's address, I beg you, because the
first thing I shall do on leaving this place will be to have a hat
made there.

And how about your pleasures, Monsieur Quiros?

> *Qui, de Bacchus, ou de l'Amour,*
> *Remporte aujourd'hui la victoire?*
> *Qui! . . de les fêter tour à tour*
> *Voulez-vous obtenir la gloire?*

I believe you are very capable of that, and the wines of Meursault, Chablis, the Hermitage, Côte-roti, Lanerte, Romanée, Tokay, Paphos, Sherry, Montepulciano, Falern and Brie tickle your organs lubricously for the chaste thighs of demoiselles Pamphale, Aurora, Adelaide, Rosette, Zelmire, Flora, Fatima, Pouponne, Hyacinth, Angelica, Augustina, and Fatmé. Wonderful, Monsieur Quiros! Believe me, that's how one should spend one's life; and when the author of Nature caused vines to be born on the one hand and c——s on the other, you can be quite certain that we were meant to enjoy them.

Because, as far as I am concerned, Monsieur Quiros, I too have my little pleasures, and if they are not so exciting as yours, they are no less subtle; I walk up and down; and to enliven my table (and that for a special favour) I have a man who regularly – and I am not exaggerating – takes ten pinches of snuff, sneezes half a dozen times, wipes his nose a dozen, spits and clears his throat noisily and expectorates at least another fourteen times – all inside half an hour. Don't you think that that is very *suitable* and recreative, above all when I am subjected to all the winds? . . . It is true that for my distraction a tall disabled soldier comes every fortnight to bring me a warrant to sign again, and once a year monsieur le lieutenant Charles arrives on the scene to play *the insolent* as a signal. Come, Monsieur Quiros believe me, these ecstasies are as good as yours; yours debase you into every vice, mine lead to all the virtues. Ask Madame la Présidente de Montreuil whether there is in the whole world a better method than that of bolts and bars to lead to virtue? I know very well that there are animals – like yourself, Monsieur Quiros (if you will forgive me) – who say and maintain that one can try prison once and that if it is not successful, it is very dangerous to try it again. But this statement is a bloomer, Monsieur Quiros. This is how you should reason : prison is the only remedy we know in France; so it follows that prison cannot fail to be good; and since prison is good, it must be used for every case. But it has not succeeded either the first, second or third time 'Oh well,' they reply, it is a good reason for trying it a fourth; it is not prison which is wrong, since we have just not only proved but established, that it was good, but rather the subject, and therefore he must be put back. Bleeding is good for fever; we know no better cure in France; bleeding therefore is the sovereign cure. But, Monsieur Quiros, the patient who has delicate nerves or thin blood does not get better by bleeding : some other remedy must be found. 'Not at all!' your doctor will retort, 'bleeding is excellent for fever; we have established that. Monsieur Quiros has a fever : so he must be bled.' And this is what is known as *powerful* reasoning. . . . To that people much more sensible than you, Monsieur Quiros, who are a clodhopper, (I ask your pardon) say : 'Pagans, atheists, blasphemers! how can you confuse the illnesses of the body with those of the soul? Don't you feel that there is no connection between the body and the soul? and the proof, is that your soul, whoremonger and drunkard that you are, belongs to the devil while your body is in a cell at Saint-Eustache.' There is therefore a very great difference between the soul and the body : therefore one cannot establish any conformity between the procedure for the cures of one and that of the other. Further, I a doctor, gain by letting your blood : I get so much for every jab of the lancet; so you have to be bled. And I, Sartine, gain by having you put in prison; I get so much a prisoner, therefore you must be shut away. What do you say to this logic, Monsieur Quiros? Come, believe me, you would be well advised to shut up and stop coming here to make your repeated objections; prison is the monarchy's finest institution. . . . If I had not kept my son-in-law in prison, the *Présidente de Montreuil* will tell you, would I have been able to marry the 5's, 3's and 8's, could I have fixed up some 23's and 9's? so arrange things that at the first visit my daughter makes to her husband, at her last and when she finally comes to collect him, more than 80 figures will turn out the same? Eh, you clod, the *Présidente* will proceed, could I have done that if I had sought the happiness of my son-in-law, the cure of his mind or his restoration to the path of virtue? And are not combinations of figures worth all the foolish procedures you advise me? Happiness, virtue, head-cures, we see these things everyday. But sets of figures, resemblances, only my favourite Albaret and myself are capable of working those things out. At this profound reasoning, Monsieur Quiros, your arms will drop to your side, your smile will extend to your ears, your right eyebrow will move over to the left, your nose will swell, you will become knock-kneed and you will cry out in your enthusiasm, 'Ah, I always said that this bitch had greater wit than me, and my cousin Albaret likewise! Come, Monsieur Quiros, cough, blow your nose, spit, fart, and intone for me : 'Margot has gone to the prison hulks.'

NOTES

1 Lieutenant-General of the Police.
2 De Maupéou had presided over the court which gave judgement in the Rose Keller affair and by a coincidence was Président of the Parlement of Aix when de Sade was condemned to death in his absence. (*Ed.*)
3 Madeleine-Laure, de Sade's only daughter, 1771–1844.
4 Charles de Rougemont, governor of the Château de Vincennes.
5 Molé, famous actor at the Théâtre Français.
6 Three fortress-prisons. (*Trans.*)
7 See Introduction for reference to numbers. (*Trans.*)

LETTER VII

MY LONG LETTER
To Madame de Sade

I truly believe, my dear wife, that your purpose would be to inculcate in me the same respect for your divinities as that with which you yourself are so deeply imbued. And since you are going to crawl before all this gang, you would have me do likewise! Would that a ***, a ***, a *** and a *** were gods for me as they are for you! If you are unlucky enough to have that idea lodged in your head, I beg you to get rid of it forthwith. Misfortune will never debase me;

> *'Je n'ai point dans les fers pris le coeur d'un esclave,'*[1]
>
> (Les Arsacides)

Nor will *I* ever take a slave's heart. Were these wretched chains to lead me to the grave, you will always see me the same. I have the misfortune to have received from Heaven a resolute soul which has never been able to yield and will never do so. I have absolutely no fear of offending anyone. You give me too many proofs that my time is fixed for me to doubt it: consequently it depends on no one to increase or diminish it. Furthermore, even if this were not so, I should never depend on all these people. It would be on the King – he is the only person in the realm whom I respect – he and the Princes of the Blood. Below them I see everything so much in bulk, all so prodigiously equal that the best thing that I can do in the circumstances is not to try and look too deeply into it because as I should feel superiority on my side, my present deep disgust would merely find more solid buttresses.

You are evidently aware that it is beyond belief that they should wish to treat me as in fact they do and expect me not to complain; for, finally, let us reason for a moment: when a term of imprisonment has to be as long as mine, is it not a real scandal that they should wish to increase the horror with all the torments it has pleased your mother to invent? Is it not enough that I should be deprived of everything that makes life sweet and agreeable; is it not enough not to be able to breathe fresh air, and see all one's wishes continually dashed against four walls and only such days go by as will await us when we are in the grave? This terrible torture is not enough according to this horrible creature: it has to be increased further by everything her imagination can devise to redouble its horror. You will admit that there is only one monster capable of taking vengeance to such a point. . . . 'But' you will reply, 'it is your imagination; things like that are not done; they are figments of the brain such as come to people in your situation.' Figments? Well, from my notebook in which I record my thoughts – in which are now 56 proofs like the one I am about to quote – I will choose just one, and you shall judge whether it is not an envenomed fury that dictated all the devices that this odious termagant has caused to be carried out here, and whether they can be dismissed as 'figments'.

You must not doubt for a moment that whatever reasons a prisoner may have for expecting a very lengthy term, the slightest measures which seem to him to favour an earlier release are seized on by him with incredible eagerness: it is human nature, there's nothing wrong in it; thus, he should not be punished but pitied. It is therefore a manifest piece of cruelty to foment, engender and produce any moves which lead him into error. One should take the greatest pains to do the opposite, and humanity (if there were any here) should continually put it into men's hearts not to aggravate in this way the most sensitive feeling of the wretched victims; for it is clear that suicides are always merely the result of hope deceived. Therefore one must not build up such a hope when it is not destined to be fulfilled, and whoever does so is a monster. Hope is the most sensitive part of a poor wretch's soul; whoever raises it only to torment him is behaving like the executioners in Hell who, they say, incessantly renew old wounds and concentrate their attention on that area of it that is already lacerated. Yet this is precisely what your mother has been doing to me during the last four years: hopes crowding on hopes as one month follows the next. To hear these people talk, and read your notes and letters etc. I should be on the eve of my discharge; then, when the 'eve' arrives, suddenly a fresh dagger-thrust and a *good drawn-out farce*. This disagreeable woman appears to find it diverting to arouse the desire in me to build castles of cards for the sheer pleasure of knocking them down once they are made. Apart from all the risks that my hope incurs thereby, the chance of wrecking it and the certainty of undermining it for the rest of my life, there is, as you will readily admit, the much more imminent danger of producing the final excess of despair. And, at present I have no reason to doubt for one moment that such is not her sole aim and that, failing to have me killed by leaving me for five years in the terrible situation in which I found myself prior to my imprisonment, she decided to work at it perhaps another five years in a more persistent manner. From the host of proofs that I have just mentioned concerning this little barbarous amusement she finds in raising and destroying my hopes, I will quote a more recent one in order to convince you. About six months have gone by since you sent me a curtain for my room; I pleaded with them in vain to hang it; they refuse. What conclusion am I to draw? *It is simply not worth it*. That is how my hope is raised; that's how things will remain up to the time when they imagine that we have been able to build a castle. When that time arrives they will come along and hang it – and the castle will be demolished. That is the kind of amusement Madame la Présidente de Montreuil indulges in; such has been her gentle occupation for the last four years with the minions she bribes to serve her in these kindnesses and who make fun of her – at least, judging by what Marais, jealous doubtless at being left out of the number – has assured me – once they have received her presents or her money. She has now carried out 56 of these manœuvres, no fewer, not counting those to come; not that I hold 56 different opinions as to how to get out of here. God forbid! Or else I would have spent my whole life in counting and I have been far from doing so (have you not proof of my more serious occupations?) but I have noted very carefully and have thereby concluded that it is probable that instead of the fourth castle in Spain – which is what I have come to and one which doubtless, however remote it is at present, will collapse like the other three; instead of the fourth, I repeat, she had plotted to make me want to build 56 by now! Now, I ask you; is that the conduct of a sensible woman, an intelligent woman and a woman who, were it only because of the ties that unite us, should be alleviating my troubles instead of adding to them? But, you say, she is offended. In the first place, I deny it : she has been injured only because she herself insisted on it. She has only her temperament to blame for everything that she regards as a personal insult. But assuming that she has in fact been hurt : should she seek vengeance? A pious woman like her who outwardly appears to perform all the formalities of religion, should she scorn the first and most essential of all Christian teachings? Let us assume vengeance on her part; I insist on that. Well and good; is not so long and arduous a prison sentence sufficient vengeance for her? Does it need increasing? *'Oh! you don't understand, you add; it was all necessary; it is why we have won.'* 'Won!' In the name of all that's good, supposing I were to leave prison tomorrow, would you dare say that *I* have won, without being afraid

that I should accuse you of an intolerable insolence? 'Won!'
put someone in prison four or five years for an 'orgy with girls'
of which there are eighty similar ones in Paris every day of the
year, and then come and tell him he is lucky to get off with
five years' imprisonment and that if he has been handled the
way they've handled him, it was 'to win'! No, I dismiss this
idea; I find it too revolting, and I am sure that you will never
have the effrontery to support it.

Let us for a moment go back on our tracks, and repeat the
phrase a *mere wenching orgy;* it is one that I can see from
here startles those who regret their inability to convince me of
all the imputations they accept against me. All my adventures
can be reduced to three. I will say nothing about the first: it
wholly concerns Madame La Présidente de Montreuil; and if
anyone should be punished it should be she herself.² But in
France they do not punish people who have a hundred thousand *livres* income, and below them are set small victims
whom they can offer to those voracious monsters who live on
sucking the blood of unfortunate victims. They ask for their
small victims; they are handed over; they are satisfied. That is
why I am in prison. The second adventure is the Marseilles
affair.³ I think it is useless to say anything about that one either.
It has been ascertained, I believe, that the offence was no worse
than debauchery and the criminal element they thought they
had better add by way of satisfying the vengeance of my
enemies in Provence and the rapacity of the Chancellor who
wanted to give his son my job was pure invention. Thus I
consider that the adventure in question was more than can-
celled out by my imprisonment at Vincennes and exile from
Marseilles.

Let us pass on to the third. I ask your pardon in advance for
the terms I am forced to use; I will tone them down as best
as I can by abridging them. In any event, between husband
and wife one can, when necessary, express oneself a little more
freely than with strangers or mere friends. I also beg your

forgiveness for these confessions, but I would rather that you thought of me as a libertine than as a criminal. Here is the plain truth about my offence and I am not disguising it one iota.

Seeing myself reduced to passing my time alone in a very remote castle, almost always without your company and suffering from the trifling weakness (I must confess) of being a little too fond of women, I applied to a very well-known procuress in Lyon and said: I want to take three or four servant-girls home with me; I want them young and pretty; supply me with them. The said procuress, Nanon, for Nanon was the recognized procuress in Marseilles[4] – I will prove it when proof is required – promises me the girls and sends them. I go off with them; I use them. Six months later, some parents come along to demand their return, assuring me that they are their children. I give them back, and suddenly a charge of abduction and rape is brought against me. It is a monstrous injustice. The law on this point is – and I have it from M. de Sartine who was kind enough to explain it to me himself one day as he may remember – as follows: it is expressly forbidden in France for any procuress to supply virgin maidens, and if the girl supplied is a virgin and lodges a complaint, it is not the man who is charged but the procuress who is punished severely on the spot. But even if the male offender has requested a virgin he is not liable to punishment: he is merely doing what all men do. It is, I repeat, the procuress who provided him with the girl and who is perfectly aware that she is expressly forbidden to do so, who is guilty. Therefore this first charge against me in Lyon of abduction and rape, was entirely illegal; I have committed no offence. It is the procuress to whom I applied who is liable to punishment – not I. But they cannot get anything out of the procuress and the girls' parents hope to extract some money from me. Let's pass on. Originally I had an adventure at Arcueil in which a woman who proved both a liar and a cheat had, with the purpose of gaining money (which was foolishly paid), spread the rumour all over Paris that I was carrying out experiments, and that my garden was a graveyard in which I buried the corpses which I had used for my purposes. This rumour was only too useful : it served my enemies' fury too well for them to resist the temptation to dish it up in every shape in any matters that might concern me. As a result, in the Marseilles affair, it was of course another of my 'experiments', an experiment that I insisted on carrying out, and also an experiment carried out on girls who were destined to disappear. But if they have not all reappeared in Lyon, they have not failed to turn up in other parts of the world. Let us look more closely into the matter. There were five of these girls from Lyon; it is a known fact. One of them was frightened by the solitude in which she was kept (not for the purpose of experiments but because decency obliged me) and ran away to my uncle. *Her fate is known.* One stayed openly in my service and died a respectable death in it, as is common knowledge in the whole province; her body was duly on view in the village and properly looked after by the director of public health. *So her fate is known.* Two have been restored to their parents. *So their fate is known.* Finally the fifth, loudly threatening to run away like her friend and talk if she was kept in solitude any longer, since she had no parents clamouring for her, was handed over by me to a peasant at La Coste (whom I will name when the time comes and whom you know very well) to be sent out in service with one of the said peasant's relations; and as I possess all the proofs, I must confess that it will give me great pleasure to show them when necessary. She was escorted there, settled in and left, and the correct certificate was brought back to me and it is now in my safe-keeping likewise ready to be shown when the need arises. I have since heard that this creature has left that service to become a p——. There then is the existence of the five girls from Lyon set down so clearly that I defy the most skilled or rather the wiliest lawyer to prove to me anything to the contrary.

Let us continue the story. Three other girls of an age and position not to be demanded back by their parents, likewise lived some weeks before or after in the castle of La Coste. Let us follow out their fate and may this be a full confession, for it is my intention, and wish, if possible, to destroy beyond all doubt the faintest hint of all the horrors they have been pleased to invent against me and which have caused Mme de Montreuil to treat me as she does, both because of her extreme credulity and the weapons the scandal supplies to her vengeance.

The first of these three girls was called *Du Plan;* she was a dancer at the Comédie de Marseille. She made no secret of living in the castle in her own name and under the title of 'housekeeper'; she also left it openly. More than a year later I found her again at the Comédie de Bordeaux and she still lived in a small provincial town which was mentioned to me at the time of my journey to Aix. No need, therefore, for any anxiety about that girl. The second came from Montpellier; she was called *Rosette*. She remained hidden away in the castle for about two months. After a while, she grew bored and expressed a wish to go, so we arranged together for her to write to a man she knew at Montpellier. This man, who was a carpenter by trade, and I believe, her host in the said town of Montpellier, was to come and collect her at the foot of the castle walls. The hour, the place, the day, the rendezvous – everything was explained. On the day agreed the man arrived and the girl was delivered into the hands of the said man by me in person while the girl named *Marie* (the girl from Lyon who was still in my service) carried her bundle which was likewise handed to the man. He proceeded to set the girl and her bundle on the mule he had brought; he received six golden *louis* from me which the girl begged me to hand him – the wages she had gained in my service – and off they went. This event took place in June 1775. In October 1776, I went to spend a fortnight in Montpellier from which I brought back the third girl in question. The girl called Rosette certainly

existed in Montpellier at that time, the proof is that I saw her
there, *saw her in every way, or more accurately, in the full
extent of the term,* and she it was who persuaded the third,
called Adelaide, to come and do as she had done, assuring her
in the presence of two or three women who will possibly not all
be absent when I am in a position to speak, assuring her, I
repeat, that, apart from loneliness, she would have no cause
for anything but self-congratulation on my treatment of her. It
was solely on her recommendation that I obtained the other
who, not knowing me, would certainly not have come otherwise. So Adelaide arrived and stayed with me up to the time of
Mme de Montreuil's third scandal, when the postmaster of
Courthézon took her back. So there we have the fate of the
third authenticated. Two or three other girls, some as cooks,
some as kitchen maids, among whom were those we brought to
Paris, have at various periods of my absence lived in the castle
of La Coste. But they spent so little time there and came and
went so openly that I think it is useless to talk about the matter.
A niece of that procuress Nanon whom we have just dis-
cussed was one of their number and we packed her off to a
convent. Mme de Montreuil has got her out; so she knows
what has happened to her. That is all. You have my full confession as I should make it before God if I was on the point of
death.

What are the conclusions to be drawn from all this? That
M. de Sade who is doubtless considered guilty of every kind
of horror since he has been kept in prison so long and who has
every reason to fear it, both for the reason that he is about to
reveal, and because twice he has experienced the power of the
evil calumny of the public against him, is however no more
guilty of *tests* and *experiments* or of *murders* in this last affair
than in any of the others, that M. de Sade has done what the
whole world does, he has seen girls who were either already
corrupted or supplied by a procuress, and therefore there is no
case of seduction against him, and that nevertheless M. de Sade

is being punished and made to suffer as if he were guilty of the blackest crimes.

Let us now examine the proofs that are brought against him :

1. *The admission of the guilty procuress:* but are not the personal reasons which she had for justifying herself strong enough to suggest that, as far as she could, she accused the person she believed to be her accomplice?

2. *The non-existence of the girls:* I am prepared to wager my head on it and lose it without regret if it is proved.

3. *The human bones discovered in the garden:* they were brought by the girl whose name is Du Plan; she is hale and hearty enough – you can interrogate her; the joke – whether a good or bad one I leave to you to judge – consisted of decorating a little room with the bones; they were truly used for that and buried in the garden when the joke – or piece of stupidity – was over. They can count the bones and compare what they discover with the receipt I have from Mademoiselle Du Plan concerning the number and kind she brought from Marseilles : you will soon see whether they can unearth a single one more. All these verifications and comparisons however are indispensable to a story of this sort. But have they gone to the pains of making even one? No! Indeed, it was not the truth that they were after, but getting me put in prison – and here I am. But perhaps some day I will be released and then perhaps they will do me the justice of conceiving that I shall be able to justify myself and see all those who mete out such treatment condemned in their turn; or at any rate if success is denied me because money and patronage is on their side, at any rate, I repeat, I shall cover them publicly with ignominy, shame and confusion.

To continue; I do not want to leave any stone unturned. What will be their additional proof? A child's testimony? But this was a servant : thus, in his capacity as a child and as a servant he cannot be believed. Furthermore, another interest is discernible here : this child depended on a very interested

mother, one who believed that by persuading him to recount
a thousand horrors she would gain a guaranteed income. She
knew about the hundred *louis* from Arcueil.[5] But they will
object perhaps: *'How do you know that the testimony of this
child was against you? He had seen things then and he knew
therefore, since you appear to be afraid of his statements?'*
This is what I expected from you, and it is precisely around
that that the whole infamous intrigue is being built up. First of
all, who should fear it, knowing that he was going to be inter-
rogated in the same way and by people of the same kind as
those who had previously made a row at Lyon? This is the
first reason why I should be mortally afraid he might invent
things as they have done and for the same purpose. But that
is not the whole story, and I will tell you what I learned and
has been told me on my journey in Provence by a man who
seemed far too much in the know for me to suspect him of
inventing it. I have given my word of honour never to com-
promise him and nothing will induce me to name him. But I
also give my word that this secret cannot be kept for ever. If
he should be dead when I come out, I shall be released from
my word and I shall name him; if he is still alive I can almost
guarantee that I shall be able to persuade him to release me
from my oath of secrecy, and then you will hear what it is. I
am going to put his own words into his own mouth to make
them more effective: 'You have everything to fear, Monsieur,'
he said, 'even when your Aix affair is over. The child you had
with you as a secretary in 1775 was, on emerging from the
castle, left with his mother in houses at Aix to be at the disposal
of the General Prosecutor and there, I can assure you as
positively as if I had heard it myself, they prompted both of
them. As once your affair was over M. de Castillon[6] was afraid
you would attack his cousin, M. de Mende,[7] who set in motion
that iniquitous procedure at Marseilles against you, uneasy about
everything he had heard about it in Paris, and unable either
to guess or know your intentions and seeing that the said M.

de Mende would be ruined if you produced counter-accusations, was very glad to be forewarned against you. So a tissue of horrors were dictated to mother and child; they were given money and they said and wrote everything that was required. Next, M. de Castillon, to lend himself the air of a man who, far from looking for wounds and bumps, was content to temporize, informed your mother-in-law and they arranged between them to pack mother and child off to Paris, so well paid, so full of hope for the future and so well primed that it is highly probable they have maintained the same things in Paris as were drilled into them in Aix.' That is what I have been told, I give you my word of honour, and told by someone who was certainly in a position to know. Whatever may happen I claim that I shall be able to obtain permission from him to name him one day, and you shall see whether or not I force him to it.

Thus I have against me in so vital an affair a procuress in my service and a child, likewise in my service; a procuress whose principal interest is to be exonerated at my expense and a child who has been obviously won over by my greatest enemies. A simple reflection here, independent of all my assertions, if you please : have you not had proofs as clear as day that they were well versed in how best to bring about my ruin at Aix when they wanted? Since you have had these proofs as clear as day in a first affair in the said town of Aix, why do you wish to refuse to believe those that may well exist in the second? You will agree that this assumption is a strong one and very much in my favour. Tell me this : would you care to enter a wood where your purse had been taken a first time? And if they took it on a second occasion, would you not feel more than justified in believing that the thieves were the same in both cases? If I had been Mme de Montreuil, that fact alone would have sufficed to make me turn down all the denunciations against my son-in-law if they came from that town.

Let us pursue the matter; there is still another point that I am anxious to settle. They have found or could find three

objects in my wallet that tell against me. Let me account for all
three. One was a recipe for delivering a pregnant woman who
was anxious to get rid of her fruit. It was wrong of me and no
doubt an indiscreet action on my part to have collected such
a thing, I agree. I can assure you that I have never used it and
did not take it with the idea of ever using it. In my life I have
had occasion to see two or three women or girls–I won't
specify–who had very strong reasons for concealing the results
of their immoral conduct with their lovers and for resorting
to such a crime. They have admitted as much to me and at the
same time they revealed the extremely dangerous methods that
those skilled in the art used on them and in which it seems to
me they risked their lives. As I heard in Italy about this method
as described on the paper in my wallet, and thought it very
mild and without any risk, I copied it down out of curiosity. I
think that no reasonable man would consider there was anything to make a fuss about, and there is not a choirboy who
is unaware that savin has the same effect.

The second piece of paper was the result of an argument
with the little doctor of Rome. He claimed that the Ancients
poisoned their swords by the method he dictated to me; I maintained a contrary opinion, telling him that I believed that I
was sure I had read somewhere about a different method. The
matter arose from some antique weapons we had seen together
at the armoury of the Castel Sant' Angelo. As I was eager to
include a few words about the subject in my description of
Rome, I took down his opinion, promising to send him my own
as soon as I had found it, and then, in my dissertation, to decide
which was the more probable. In point of fact I discovered this
opinion contradictory to his own in one of the books you sent
me, the fourth volume of the *History of the Celts*.[8] It concerned
a plant called *linveum* and according to Pliny and Aulus-Gellius,
Hellebore, which the Ancients used to rub on their swords
when they wanted to poison the blades. I would have decided
in favour of this opinion contradicting the one which I had

been given. That was the object they discovered in that connection. Is that a venial sin then?

But now we come to the most important: a full enquiry concerning very similar matters to those with which you are accused. Yes, here we have a terrible proof but one can say that it is the story of the magpie's mass[9] all over again; I expect you know it? Well, may the latter, the Calas affair and many other similar ones teach you who imprison so lightly that you must never judge by appearances and punish people without giving them a hearing in a country which in its laws and government considers itself exempt from inquisitive vexations; and that, in short, there is not a single citizen whom you have the right to lock up without hearing him first, or who has not subsequently the right of avenging himself in any way he thinks fit provided he punishes you for your omission. Yes; whoever you are, get hold of this idea and hear what I have to say on this extremely important document. The said document is the confession of the crimes of a poor wretch who, like myself, sought refuge in Italy. He had no intention of returning to France; and seeing me prepared to cross the Alps he handed me the legal opinion of his inquiry in person, begging me to show it in France and send him the reply. I gave him my word. Two days later he came and implored me to return the document containing his writing which would be, he said, a proof against him; he wanted to have it transcribed but he could not find anyone there who knew French. So I copied it all out in my hand, solely for the satisfaction of obliging him and failed to consider the possible fate of the said paper. That then is another fact which I swear on my honour to be true and for which I will provide more definite proofs when occasion demands.

These are then all my so-called offences, the objections I intend to make and what I shall prove, I swear, by proofs and methods of such authenticity that it will be absolutely impossible to refute their evidence. I am guilty of nothing more than simple libertinage such as it is practised by all men more or less according to their natural temperaments or tendencies. Every man has his weaknesses; comparisons are odious: my gaolers themselves would perhaps not gain by a parallel. Yes, I admit that I am a libertine; I have devised everything that can be done in that line, but I have not practised all that I have devised and I never intend to do so. I may be a libertine but I am neither a criminal nor a murderer, and since they force me to produce my apology side by side with my justification, I will add that it might well be that those who condemn me so unjustly would find it difficult to offset their infamies by laudable actions as well authenticated as those to which I can oppose my misdemeanours. I am a libertine, but three families domiciled in your quarter have lived five years on my alms and I have saved them from the worst extremities of poverty. I am a libertine, but I have saved a deserter from death when he had been abandoned by his whole regiment and his colonel. I am a libertine, but in the eyes of all your family at Evry and at the peril of my life I saved a child who was on the point of being crushed under the wheels of a cart drawn by runaway horses by hurling myself at them. I am a libertine, but I have never compromised my wife's health. I have never indulged in other aspects of libertinage such are often so fatal to the family fortunes. Have I ever ruined my children through gambling or other extravagances which might one day have deprived them or encroached on their inheritance? Have I mismanaged my estate while it was at my disposal? Did I in fact ever give any hint in my youth of a heart capable of all the blackness which my enemies at present assume? Have I not always shown regard towards all the people I ought to love and cherished all who had claims on my affection? Did I not love my father? (alas, I still weep for him every day). Have I behaved badly towards my mother, and was it not when I was hearing her last sighs and paying her my last respects that yours caused me to be dragged into this foul prison where she leaves me to languish for four years? In a word, examine my life from my childhood days onward. You have about you two persons who have followed its course, Amblet and Mme de Saint-Germain.[10] Passing on from that to my youth which was observed by the Marquis de Poyanne[11] under whose eyes I spent it, proceed to the age at which I got married and see, enquire and discover whether I have ever given proofs of the barbarity which I am supposed to have and whether any ill-considered acts have fore-shadowed the crimes which are attributed to me : that must be the case for there are as you know various degrees of crime. How then do you suppose that from so innocent a childhood and youth, I have suddenly reached the ultimate heights of calculated horror : no, you do not believe it. And you who tyrannize over me so cruelly today, you do not believe it either : your desire for revenge has warped your judgement, you have surrendered to it blindly, but your heart knows me; it made a fairer judgement, and is well aware that it is innocent. One day I shall have the pleasure of seeing you agree, but the admission can never compensate me for my present torments, nor shall I have suffered any the less. . . . In a word, I want my name cleared as it will be when they choose to release me from here. If I am a murderer I shall not have been here long enough; if I am not, I shall have been too severely punished and will have the right to claim compensation.

You will think this is a very long letter. But it is one I owed to myself and that I promised myself I would write one day when my four years of suffering had gone round. They have now expired. Here then is the letter; written as if I was on the point of death, so that if I should suddenly die before I have the comfort of taking you in my arms once more, I may with my dying breath refer you to the feelings expressed in the present letter, as to the last ones that a heart anxious to take at least your good opinion to the tomb will address to you. You will forgive its confusion; it is neither elegant nor witty. I am striking out some names I put at the beginning so that it will reach you and it is my earnest wish that it may. I do not expect you to reply to me in detail, but merely to let me know that you have received 'my long letter' for that is how I shall style it, yes, that is how I shall style it. And when I refer you back to the sentiments it expresses you will re-read it. . . . Do you hear, my dear wife? You will re-read it and see that the one who will love you to the grave wished to sign it with his blood.

DE SADE

This 20th February.

(Note enclosed)

It rarely happens that I write such lengthy letters, nor any so necessary to my justification; and it will certainly not happen again. In consequence I beg those through whose hands it will pass to make sure my wife receives it. I trust they will, and not justify my fear that they withhold letters of no less importance than this, in a word, letters in which I justify myself; for if they withheld them and prevented their circulation, they would agree that I would then be authorised to lodge a justifiable complaint of their conduct and reveal it by proving the well-established interest that they doubtless had in my imprisonment since they opposed any means I had of putting forward my justification for having my period of detention curtailed.

NOTES

1 *Les Arsacides,* a six-act tragedy in verse by Peyrayd de Beaussol, was performed at the Théâtre Français on 26th July 1775. (*Trans.*)

2 The Rose Keller affair.

3 The 'poisoned sweets' affair.

4 Monsieur Lély has stated in his notes to *L'Aigle, Mademoiselle* that this assertion should be accepted with caution. (*Ed.*)

5 The payment made to Rose Keller by the Montreuil family.

6 M. Le Blanc de Castillon, *avocat-général* to the Parlement of Aix.

7 Procurator-royal at the Seneschal court of Marseilles.

8 *Histoire des Celtes et particulièrement des Gaulois et des Germains,* published 1740–1750, and written by Simon Pelloutier, minister of the French church in Berlin. (*Ed.*)

9 A mass said in memory of the condemnation of a maid-servant, innocent of a theft committed by a magpie at Palaiseau. (*Trans.*)

10 Possibly a relative of the Comte de Saint-Germain, war minister in 1775. (*Ed.*)

11 A senior officer in the cavalry regiment to which de Sade had belonged as a young man.

LETTER VIII

To Madame de Sade

(Vincennes, 21st May 1781)

Nothing could be more agreeable than your little arrangement, but you do not sufficiently conceal its wickedness : for that is all I discover in it. Otherwise it would be delightful. Let us take a closer look. You (or your agents) are eager to make some arrangement that palliates or ends my troubles; but you are uncertain about the outcome of the said arrangement. It may be good, it may be bad : well, why talk to me about it? You should leave me as I was and go your way. If your scheme came off, you could report to me the step taken at the same time as its success. If it failed? I should remain as I was. There it is then; if everything you say you have done was true – what common sense in fact dictates in such a case – that is certainly what you would have done. Any steps contrary to that reveal the deceit behind the complication and show the whole thing to be a ruse which I fortunately saw through straight away. I told you so on the 3rd or 4th April and I have not changed much since then. Yet M. Le Noir's visit was intended to have that effect. A magistrate whom one supposed respectable and who comes and announces : 'Your troubles are over, your misdeeds are expiated', has a right to be taken at his word. He deceived me. Well, what is the result? He has lowered himself much more than I have, for there is a great deal of difference between the victim and the rogue and certainly not to the advantage of the deceiver.

However, there is one consistent feature about it all : magistrates, parents, business men, friends, *valets or commandant* (it's the same thing), all agree to speak on the same note; the instrument has only one string; it is played with equal skill by them all. Some (I am referring to those I have underlined), like the good, clumsy dolts that they are, the rest with a little more art, but unison is everything; they all agree that '*he must be lied to and lied to basely.*' That is the outcome. It is still the letter of the comte de La Tour which I discovered at the commandant de Miolans's : '*The intention of the Présidente de Montreuil, who has obtained permission from the minister to manage everything to do with the Marquis de Sade, is that the latter should be deceived from morning till night; consequently you must never stop telling him that his affair is about to come to an end.*' It is clear, then, from these sinister intrigues that the plan for my punishment has been and is to deceive me and fool me for ten or twelve years. Now, my reply is this : there is and can only be one hypocrite, one cheat and one rogue as infamous as Monsieur de S.[1] Who can have advised such horrible treatment, only one blackguard – capable of having more than two hundred innocent people, free or in chains, done to death – from whom such advice could emanate. The odious monster was not satisfied with ruining me from my childhood days on, he further desires to see the last chapter of my life resemble the first so that right to the end he would be able to congratulate himself on having been its executioner, this man who deserves the tortures of Damiens[2] since with his well-known plot he thought to overturn the State, this man who caused a poor wretch, known to be innocent to be broken on the wheel, a man who could not possibly have been guilty and who died saying : '*I denounce the infamy of my judge before the throne of God who will be my judge*' – remarkable words which, were I King, I should make him have engraved on his coach, that is if he ever decided to have one by way of proving his superiority over his ancestors who were only too pleased to earn a few sous by beating up miserable prisoners of the Inquisition in Madrid. This is the swine with whom I have to deal, the loathsome person to whom they appealed and to whom your odious mother was all the more enchanted to have recourse because she knew he was my sworn enemy and would tender her only such advice as could flatter her revenge.

Any punishment that does not correct, that can merely rouse rebellion in whoever has to endure it, is a piece of gratuitous infamy which makes those who impose it more guilty in the eyes of humanity, good sense and reason, nay a hundred times more guilty than the victim on whom the punishment is inflicted. The axiom is too self-evident to be refuted. Now, what can you hope for? And what do you dare flatter yourself that you obtain from all that except to ruin my character and humour and turn me into a cheat, a rogue and a villain like the rest of you? For, finally, whether the comparison fits or not, you must concede that it is a just one : but what you are doing is exactly what people do to dogs to make them more vicious. *'Oh! we will always bring you back when it suits us! All we shall need to do is to talk to you about your release; that is what we wanted to see when we sent M. Le Noir² to you. You were as gentle as a lamb, because he came to flatter you.'* That is your system, isn't it? Well, put your trust in it! That's all that I can say.

In a word, there are plenty of examples of offences like mine but there is not a single one of the type you have used to persecute me. It is iniquitous and illegal from every point of view, it cannot have been recommended either by the King or sovereign court and it will consequently leave me every right to demand revenge or – following your example – to take it myself if they refuse.

I do not need to ask to see M. Le Noir. I still venerate him enough not to want to burden his conscience with a further injustice against me. One day he will be grateful to me. As for you, it is different; I have the greatest desire to see you. Since you first mentioned it you must have had consent or refusal on hundreds of occasions. I warn you therefore that if I do not see you before the Whitsun festival I shall be convinced that the whole thing is a farce, that I am about to be released and I shall make my preparations accordingly. Thus, consider what you want me to believe about that. Either come, or I conclude that I am leaving; that is clear. M. Le Noir has not changed, nothing has changed, and for the last ten years everything has been arranged, decreed, the days fixed, the lies decided on, the comedies learned, and all that has happened is that the whole matter has assumed somewhat larger proportions as your old hag of a mother has grown old and, abandoned by the whole world (which has never thought a great deal of her) sees herself descending to the grave. It would seem that like the snake she is bent on discharging all her venom before expiring. Well, let her hurry up, the abominable creature, even if we should be stunk out by all the rest of the poison that is left in her foul entrails. Let her hasten to breathe her last and surrender her filthy soul.

You say that my imprisonment is having a bad effect in Provence. Ah! I need little convincing; you have no need to mention it unless it is to pour a little balm on my wounds. Well, since that is the situation, how can your mother enjoy ruining the father of her grandchildren? And that being so, how do you expect me not to call her a monster unworthy of life? Whom in Provence will you now convince that the Marseilles exile was not virtually a banishment from the provinces? Oh! they took steps to prevent the people in the provinces from discussing the matter! You would be very cunning if you managed to find any that did : but I swear that it is all one to me; my intentions remain the same and have never varied. Once outside this place I shall be sheltered from the opinion my compatriots have of me, for I shall soon be a long way from them.

I have nothing to add to the messages I have sent you for Milli Rousset. Once she has waited as long as three years for me, she might as well wait another three, if that is my sentence, as borne out by the visit of M. Le Noir who always makes a habit of marking off the half-years of my sentence as he leaves. It makes me feel that I am here for centuries; and it is unworthy of her; that is all I can say to her. Do not go and answer me with 'But it is your fault if you are not out of Vincennes; you have been offered Montelimart[4] you have only to go there. . . .' Your Montelimart was all a fairy tale; it never had any foundation; and to prove it, suppose I accept to go off unconditionally, with or without escort? Let us now see what you say about that and whether or not it is a fairy tale. I am not telling you, this to see how you take it : one thing I shall always go on repeating is my request for a transfer to Montelimart and that I would rather go there (however bad it may be) than remain in this abominable prison where infamies, villainies and filth have reached such a pitch.

Now that I have got going, I might as well quote you three fresh examples. The other day I felt a craving for a piece of lamb, after all lamb is served up even on cobblers' tables at this time of year. I had to buy it with my own money. What do you think of such stinginess? Yesterday as I heard them crying green peas and so far not having had the pleasure of seeing any, I got them to send up a mash of last year's dried peas which I consumed with avidity as if they were fresh because I had felt such a deprivation. And so for twice twenty-four hours I had intolerable indigestion, whereas if they had given me sound, fresh peas, they would have done me good. Would you like a more striking example? For the last three years they have made me drink stagnant cistern water which stinks like the devil whilst there is a supply of excellent pond water of M. de Rougemont's : But this has to be paid for and to provide prisoners with it would amount to a few crowns less a year from the money this swine filches from them. Would you believe that five or six letters and as many conversations have failed to convince this notorious villain of the following piece of reasoning. Commons in this establishment consists of five dishes a day, including soup, five dishes which the devil himself would refuse for they are invariably loathsome. So that the result is that there is some left for the gaolers with whom the cook has an understanding. I said : I ask for only two of these five dishes but I beg that they should be good and have all the money spent on them you would have to spend on the five. That seems a fair arrangement to me. If my family pays six *livres* a day for my food, I have a right to ask that these six *livres,* when my laundry deduction is made, should be wholly devoted to the said two dishes, since that is all I take. If you object, Monsieur le Commandant, it means one of two things : it is either that in providing me with two courses as bad as the five you are robbing me of the three I do not take, or you are allowing your cook to conspire with your gaolers to steal them from me; there can be no alternative. Well, there you have the logic that M. de Rougemont has consistently refused to under-stand. The two courses are no improvement on the five – witness the green peas that I thought would finish me off. I implore you to lodge the strongest possible complaints about it to M. Le Noir on my behalf, or, if you do not see eye to eye with me on the subject, I will myself write him a letter which will make the comic little Rougemont blush with shame if he has any shame left. You must specify to M. Le Noir that as I drink no wine, burn no candles and wear out half as much furniture as anyone else and have no linen etc., I intend and have a right to demand that, apart from payment for my laundry, with no profit to my gaoler, all the money that comes through for my keep should be spent on the two courses that I actually eat. That should ensure that they are edible. For once again, this shrivelled runt, this puny bastard, this miserable half-caste, this quarter-English-man, this vile creature must learn that playing these tricks or getting others to play them is not the only thing in the world.

No doubt this little jester will probably reply : But it is you who cause us to play these little games; you have to pay us for our pains. To that I have two replies: first, that it is the rôle of Madame la Présidente to play tricks, since it is she who gets others to perpetrate them; and, secondly, that I advise her to pay the most meagre wage possible, for they are damnably badly executed. When one of them has some deception to carry out, he begins by turning away, unable to hold my gaze as he lies to me, and the other (he is the favourite) when he comes along to administer the little injection that his captain has confided to him that morning, always gives his comrades a dig in the ribs to let them know that he is lying, and lying under orders, that they must therefore, follow his lead in the conversation. . . . The fools! Expecting to impose on me! And the poor *Madame Présidente* busy deluding herself that her scheme will be successful! Oh! With Rougemont it is another matter; he is more subtle, he acts more convincingly. He is in fact the only one in the troupe who is worth at least twenty *sous* for each performance; one might even step it up to thirty on the days when he arrives, stuffed with food and his tongue enveloped in gobbets of matter which he belches up and splutters out: *'Oh no, I tell you! You don't do me justice. You believe that words are made for mutual understanding which is far from the truth; you must not believe a word of what I am doing myself the honour of telling you, because words have no meaning. Oh, no, I tell you. . . .'* Then he is taken with a fit of the hiccoughs and he is unable to continue. You must agree that I was very patient and took full stock of my situation to refrain from driving this joker out with kicks in the belly. But he is not going to lose thereby; I give you my word.

At any rate, may I be permitted to conclude with an axiom dictated by common sense: it is that it is not for vice and the most characteristic horror of vice to aim at reforming or punishing vice; it can be done only by virtue and the purest virtue at that. It is not for Madame la Présidente de Montreuil, cousin, niece, parent, goddaughter and foster-mother of the wickedest frauds from Cadiz to Paris, Madame la Présidente de Mon-

treuil, niece of a rogue kicked out of the Invalides by M. de
Choiseul for embezzlement and extortion, la Présidente de
Montreuil whose husband's family includes a grandfather
hanged in the Place de Grève, the Présidente de Montreuil
who has presented her husband with seven or eight bastard
sons and made whores of all her daughters; it is not for her
to exacerbate, punish or repress faults of temperament of which
one is not the master and which have never done anyone any
harm. It is not for *dom S . . . nos* who was picked up in Paris
one fine morning without anyone knowing his origins or how
he sprung into being, rather like those toadstools which suddenly spring up by the hedgeside it is not, I say, for *dom S . . .
nos* who was finally found to be the offspring, on the sinister
side, of the Reverend Father Torquemada and a Jewess seduced
by the aforesaid in the Inquisition prisons in Madrid which he
governed, *dom S . . . nos* who built up his fortune in France
solely by sacrificing men as cannibals do, and who when he was
master of the rolls and, because he prided himself on being able
to prove he was never wrong and incapable of passing false
judgement, had the poor wretch I have mentioned broken on
the wheel, *dom S . . . nos,* who, in a slightly more elevated
position, contrived vexatious and odious inroads on the
pleasures of the public in order to produce 'lascivious lists' to
warm up the little supper parties at the Parc-aux-Cerfs, and
who to pay court to each successive reigning power, did to
death, either by torture or imprisonment more than two hundred innocent persons, the calculation made by the very people
who served his infamies, *dom S . . . nos,* in short, the most
politically corrupt and most outrageous villain the sun has ever
shone on, and perhaps the first, since abuses have become
tolerated, who thought up that of keeping a whore with the
prisoners – no, it is not for such a personification of crime to
censure, criticize and acerbate offences which gave him his
most cherished pleasures in the days when he misappropriated
five hundred thousand francs a year of the million allowed him

by the King for furnishing the court with *lubricious details* and who at that time not only stole with impunity but shamefully abused his position to constrain unfortunate females to the vices which he now persecutes! I have that from the women themselves.

It is not in fact for that little bastard Rougemont, the execration of vice in person, debauchery in doublet and hose who on the one hand prostitutes his wife in order to gain prisoners and on the other starves them to gain a few more *crowns* and the means of paying the infamous backers of his debauchery, for a ridiculous squit who, but for the whims of dame fortune and the pleasure she takes in bringing low those who should be raised and elevating those who are made to crawl, who, I say, but for that, would perhaps be only too happy to be my scullion if we had both remained in the stations in which heaven had caused us to be born; it is not for a villain of this kind to cherish an ambition to set himself up as a censor of vice and the very vices which he himself possesses to an even more odious degree, because, to repeat it once more, a man becomes more ridiculous and execrable when he wants to persecute in others the faults which he possesses a hundred times worse himself, and that it is not for the halt to laugh at the lame nor the blind to offer to lead the purblind.

So be it, and I send my greetings.

NOTES

1 Gabriel de Sartine, 1729–1801, who was born in Spain, was a counsellor at the Châtelet and then rose to be Lieutenant-General of Police in 1759. Five years later he was appointed Minister of Marine. (*Ed.*)

2 Robert François of Damiens was subjected to terrible tortures for an attempt on the life of Louis XV in 1757. They are described in Peter Weiss's play, *The Persecution and Assassination of Marat as performed by the Inmates of the Asylum of Charenton under the Direction of the Marquis de Sade*. (*Trans.*)

3 Lieutenant-General of the Police; Sartine's successor.

4 The Marquise de Sade had arranged in March of 1781 for her husband to be transferred to Montélimar so that he could supervise his affairs more easily. The Marquis did not accept this transfer and later regretted his refusal.

5 Sartine.

LETTER IX

To Madame de Sade

(Vincennes, about 15th August 1781)

I am most obliged to you, my dear wife, for your solicitude in copying for me the note which I asked you for, word for word. Certainly it has calmed me down, but the hidden horrors, the complicated infamies which I have discovered in the abominable letters which your mother induced you to write and which, happily for me, I had not yet unravelled, have given me a further dose of sorrow and anxiety much stronger than that of tranquility which your own note could administer. However, despite the new perturbation I feel, and whatever my troubles and terrible apprehensions, I will look forward to your visit, hoping that your words will calm me down better than your writings, befouled as they are by your mother's bile, and that the reply you make to the questions I put – and I shall watch relentlessly your manner as you give it – I hope, I say, that this reply will be more to my benefit than a written one; and so I wait.

Thus it is ordained that you shall never calm me down about one thing without leaving me anxious about another. Why do you not reply to my urgent request that Boucher[1] should not accompany you? Can anyone compel you? However, I pass over that because it seems to me from your letter that you hope to obtain your wish and I am satisfied, to end with the subject once and for all, to repeat my solemn oath that if Boucher does accompany you and you are dollied up like a tart as you were on the last occasion, I shall refuse to come down.

When they come to find me my first question will be : *'Is Boucher there? Is she dressed like the last time?'* If the reply is in the affirmative I shall not come down, but even if it is in the negative they may be tricking me. In that case I shall come down but should I catch a glimpse of Boucher or the white dress or your transformation, I shall immediately go up again, I swear it by Almighty God and my honour; may I consider myself the biggest poltroon of all mankind if I change.

DE SADE

What is the meaning of this excuse ! *'If you saw the others!'* The others haven't their husbands in prison, or if they have and behave like that, they are tarts and only deserve insults and contempt! Tell me, would you make your Easter devotions in this mountebank or female quack costume? No, you wouldn't, would you? Well, the spirit of restraint should be the same, grief and sorrow ought to call forth in this case what piety and divine respect should evoke in the other. However *outré* the fashions may be, you will never persuade me that there are none for women of sixty. Imitate them, however distant you are from that age. Remember that my misfortune brings us close to it, if we are not already there, and that in the matter of conduct and apparel we have no choice of other fashions. If you are honest, I am the only person you should want to please; you will certainly never please me except by the appearance and *conduct* of the greatest propriety and the most perfect modesty. In short, I demand, as you love me, (and I am surely about to see the proof; the thing I am asking of you cannot be refused without completely unmasking yourself, concerning your signs, your marks and all your stupid mystification), I demand then, I repeat, that you come in the dress which you women call 'robe de chambre', in a large and high bonnet with no kind of coiffure below except your own smoothly combed hair. Not the slightest hint of false curls, chignon or false plaits; no padding and your breast unusually well covered

and not immodestly displayed as the other day; I demand that
the colour of your dress be as sober as possible. I swear to you
by all I hold most sacred that you will rouse my wrath to a
pitch of fury and that there will be a furious scene if you deviate
in the slightest from what I am prescribing. You should blush
at failing to see that the persons who got you up as you were
the other day inwardly jeered at you. Oh! they would certainly
be saying: 'the little marionette; how easily we do what we
want with her!' Be yourself for once in your life. There are
things which circumstances constrain you to be party to; but
there are others so improper and ridiculous, perhaps even so
infamous, which I am sure they wanted of you, although I
flatter myself that you refused to consent! But as for carrying
out the first and even listening to the second, you should reply
by refusing for the former and threatening to take your own
life rather than hear mention of the latter.

The fact is that I know so well what abominable hands you
are in! For, be sure of this, I am not deceived and I am perfectly aware that you are with your infamous mother; I have
so much reason to shudder, knowing you there! Yes, I do not
hesitate to say, I would prefer you to be at Madame Gourdain's![2] You would at least be mistrustful of the latter's goings-
on, whereas nothing can guarantee you against the cunning
snares which may be laid for you at the house of the other. Do
you think that I can ever forget this remark in my life: 'I
would give fifty golden louis to the man who would rob this
little hussy of her virtue'? No, I shall never forget it, and if you
wanted to collect together all the circumstances, recall the
times, places, situation, how quickly my greatest aberrations
would be explained! My dear wife, remember this, the despair
of the women who have despised virtue is the respect in which
it is held by those who have constantly honoured it; these
miserable creatures are like those would-be doubters who want
others to desecrate the god whom their hearts shudder to name.
Preserve, preserve this virtue! It is the one thing that makes me

ashamed of my lapses, it is that alone that makes me despise them. Man's natural character is to imitate; that of the sensitive man is to resemble as closely as possible the person whom he loves. It is only by imitating the vices of others that I have earned my misfortunes: do not perpetuate them by the most terrible one which could be inflicted on me. I should not survive; or if my love of life overcame my courage to kill myself (which I do not think likely), it would only be to throw myself into such a state of chaos that it might end my misery in any way conceivable as soon as possible. Inconstancy or infidelity rouse a lover or a husband, so they say; yes, if he be a debased or vile soul. But do not imagine that mine is of such a stamp. I will never forget an outrage and I shall not make any effort to take back a possession which would have ceased to belong to me. The mere idea that a woman could think of any other man when in my arms has always revolted me, and I have always refused to see again any woman whom I suspected of deceiving me. I do not think the report is true, but you have raised this suspicion in my mind and it is now rooted. What a fine piece of advice they gave you. I will delve into it; I will verify it: I shall find nothing (at least, so I hope) but the suspicion will have been sown, and in a character like mine, it works like a slow poison whose daily effects increase its ravages and nothing in the world has the power to arrest its progress. I repeat: what a fine piece of advice they gave you! It was so agreeable to anticipate a happy old age in the bosom of a faithful wife, one who had been incapable of ever failing me. It was, alas, my sole consolation, all that blunted the points that now lacerate me. And you have taken horror to the pitch of envying me this gentle hope of my old age! I can bear no more; the suspicion is sown; the phrases are only too clear for me to be blind to them. Oh, my dear wife, I shall no longer be able to esteem you! Is it true? Tell me, have you deceived me so cruelly? What a terrible future, if it be so! Great heavens, let them never open my prison! Let me die rather than emerge to perceive my shame, yours and that of the monsters who advise you! Let me die rather than leave this place to debase myself and plunge into the last excesses of the most monstrous crimes which I would plunge into for my ruin for good and all! There would be no horror I should not invent. Farewell, you see how calm I am and how much I need to see you alone. Obtain this leave I implore you.

NOTES

1 First police clerk. (*Ed.*)
2 A notorious procuress of the period.

D

LETTER X

To Mademoiselle de Rousset
A piece of philosophy for the New Year

(Vincennes 26th January 1782)

Wherever you are, mademoiselle, near or far, with Turks or Galileans, monks or actors, gaolers or honest folk, arithmeticians or philosophers, the fact is that friendship does not allow me at the start of this New Year to dispense with the sacred duties which it imposes on me – after which, in accordance with the ancient custom, I will, by your leave, give myself up to a few episodic reflections that do at any rate arise from the subject. If my situation is not free of thorns, it often prompts, I must admit, thoughts of an extremely diverting kind of philosophy.

As I think back to the period of my misfortunes, I sometimes seem to hear those seven or eight powdered wigs to whom I owe them coming back home, one from sleeping with an honest wench whom he is seducing, one from sleeping with his friend's wife, the other ignominiously escaping from some sordid street of ill-fame – for he would be extremely put out if he was discovered – another from a hovel with a still more evil reputation, I seem, I repeat, to see them all overwhelmed with luxury and infamy, sitting round the dossier of my case. And there I seem to hear the chief justice exclaim in his enthusiasm for patriotism and love of the law : 'What, my colleagues, did this little runt, who is neither a president nor master of the rolls, expect to enjoy himself like a counsellor of the Great Chamber? This little country gentleman wanted to amuse himself by imagining that he was allowed to be like one of us? Without ermine and mortier, he has got it into his head that nature was the same for him as for us! As if nature could be analysed, flouted by other people than those who interpret her laws and as if there could be any other laws than ours! Prison, 'sblood! Prison, gentlemen! That's the only possible answer. Yes, six or seven years in well-locked rooms for the impudent fellow. . . . The only way, Gentlemen, to inculcate respect for the laws of society, and the best of all remedies for anyone who has taken it into his head to violate them is to force him to curse them. There's another point too...M. de...who as you know is in office (that is, he was but is no longer, thank God), is very pleased to have the opportunity of giving his mistress a little present: the *pressurage*[1] might extract twelve or fifteen thousand francs . . . not a moment's hesitation : *'But the subject's honour . . . his wife, his goods . . . his children. . . ?* Well, Heavens above! What fine reasons those are! . . . Is that going to stop us bowing before Mammon . . . honour . . . women . . . children? Are they not victims we sacrifice every day? . . . Prison, gentlemen! prison, I tell you! And tomorrow our cousins, our brothers will become ships' captains. Prison, so be it.' President Michaut who has just had a nap replies thickly. *Prison, Gentlemen, prison!* says handsome Darval in a shrill voice as he secretly scribbles a billet-doux under his cloak to an opera girl; indisputably, prison, adds the pedagogue Damon, his head still hot from his lunch in the tavern. *Eh who can raise any doubts about prison?* Little Valère yelps in conclusion as he stands on tiptoe and glances at his watch so as not to miss his rendezvous with Mme Gourdain.

And this is what honour, life, fortune and the citizen's reputation depend on in France! Vileness, flattery, ambition, avarice begin his downfall and imbecility finishes it off.

Miserable creatures, thrown for a moment on the surface of this little pile of mud, is it decreed that one half of the flock should be the persecutor of the other? Is it for you, mankind, to pronounce on what is good and what is evil? It well becomes a puny individual of your species to undertake to set limits to nature, decide what it shall tolerate and announce what it forbids! You in whose eyes the most futile of operations is still to be resolved, you who are unable to explain the most insignificant phenomena, define to me the origin of the laws of movement, those of gravitation, elucidate the essence of matter : is it inert or not? If it does not move, tell me how nature, which is never at rest, has managed to create something which is continually in that state, and, if it moves, if it is the legitimate cause of perpetual generations and alternations, explain to me what life is and prove what death is; tell me what air is, dissertate correctly on its varying effects, tell me why I find sea-shells on mountain-tops and ruins on the sea-bed. You who decide whether a thing is a crime or not, you who have people hanged in Paris for actions that would win crowns in the Congo, fix my opinions concerning the course of the stars, their suspension, their attraction, their mobility, their composition, their phases, prove to me Newton rather than Descartes, Copernicus rather than Tycho-Brahe, just explain to me why a stone falls when it is thrown from a height, yes, put that simple fact within my grasp and I will forgive you for being a moralist when you would be a better physician. You wish to analyse the laws of nature and your heart, your heart on which it writes, is itself an enigma whose solution is beyond you! *You wish to define these laws, yet you cannot tell me how it comes about that when tiny blood-vessels get too swollen they instantly effect a person's brain and make a villain out of the most honest of men in a single day.* You, as childish in your methods as in your discoveries, you who for three or four thousand years have been inventing, changing, retrogressing, arguing, are still at the stage of offering as the reward for our virtues nothing more than the Elysium of the Greeks and for the punishment of our crimes their mythical Tartarus; you who after so much reasoning, so

many works, so many dusty volumes compiled on this sublime
subject, have progressed no further than to replace Hercules
by a slave of Titus and Minerva by a Hebrew woman, wish to
philosophize on human aberration, dogmatize on vice and
virtue, whereas it is impossible for you to explain what either
of them is, which is the most advantageous to man, which is
better suited to his nature and whether the profound equilib-
rium which makes both necessary is not perhaps the result of
this contrast. You insist that the whole universe be virtuous
and you do not feel that everything would instantly perish if
virtues alone existed on the earth; you refuse to understand
that since vices exist, it is as unjust for you to punish them as
it would be to jeer at a one-eyed man. . . . And what is the
result of your false schemes, the odious restrictions you would
like to impose on Nature which despises you? . . . Wretched
man, I shudder to say it: it is that you should break on the
wheel the man who revenges himself on his enemy and heap up
with honours the man who murders the enemies of his king,
that you should destroy the man who robs you of a crown and
seek out recompenses for yourself, you who consider yourself
justified in exterminating in the name of your laws the man
whose sole crime is that he has been carried away by those of
Nature and whose sole crime is that he was born for the sacred
preservation of his rights. Well, quit all your mad subtleties!
Enjoy life my friend, enjoy life and judge not, I say; leave it
to Nature to move you as she will and to the Eternal One that
of punishing you. If you discover that you are merely a law-
breaker, a humble ant lodged on this clod of earth, drag your
straw to the storehouse, hatch out your eggs, feed your young,
cherish them, above all do not remove the bandage of error
from their eyes: accepted fancies, I grant you, do more for
happiness than the dismal truths of philosophy. Enjoy the flame
of the universe: it is to light up pleasures, and not by sophisms,
that its light shines into your eyes. Do not waste half your life
finding ways of rendering the other half unhappy, and after

some years of vegetating in this somewhat strange form, pocket your pride and sleep awhile on mother earth and with a new identity in accordance with new laws which are as hard to understand as the first. Remember, in short, that it is to make your fellow-men happy, to care for them, help them, love them that Nature puts you in their midst, not to judge and punish them and above all not to shut them away in prison.

If this small fragment of philosophy pleases you, I shall have the satisfaction, Mademoiselle, of sending you the sequel with my next New Year greetings. Otherwise, be good enough to tell me, and we will choose some other subject more in keeping with the sprightly wit of a sex of which you are the ornament and of which I shall be proud to be all my life, as I shall of you, Mademoiselle, the very humble and obedient servant.

Des Aulnets

From the hen-run of Vincennes, this 26th January, at the end of fifty-nine and a half months of *pressurage* but which has not in fact been successful.

NOTE

1 *Pressurage:* image from wine-press. (*Trans.*)

LETTER XI

To Marie-Dorothée de Rousset
From my country house, this 17th April 1782

(Vincennes, 17th April 1782)

The eagle, Mademoiselle, is sometimes forced to leave the seventh region of the air to descend on to the top of Mount Olympus, or the ancient pines of the Caucasus, or the cold larches of the Juras, or the whitened crupper of the Taurus; sometimes even near the quarries of Montmartre. We learn from history (and history is a fine thing) that Cato, the great Cato, cultivated his fields with his own hands, that Cicero himself aligned his trees in his fine avenues at *Formies* (I do not know if anyone pruned them for him), Diogenes lived in a tub, Abraham made statues of clay, the famous author of *Télémaque*[1] wrote occasional verses for Madame Guyon, Piron sometimes left the sublime brushes of *La Métromanie*[2] to drink champagne and compose the *Ode to Priapus* (perhaps you are acquainted with this light poetic trifle, so suitable for the use of young ladies and so calculated to gain entry into any plan of education suitable for the training of the minds and hearts of those who are destined for the great, wide world?) Have we not seen the great Voltaire build a church to Our Lord with the same hand with which he wrote, speaking of the holy birth of this Redeemer :

> *Joseph, Panthere et la brune Marie*
> *Sans le savoir firent cette oeuvre pie.*[3]

103

And in our time, Mademoiselle, our own august time, do we not see the famous Madame Présidente de Montreuil quit her Euclid and her Barême to go and discuss *oil* or *salad* with her chef? All of which proves, Mademoiselle, that man strives in vain to rise above himself, there are always two fatal moments in the day which call him back to the sad condition of the beasts from which you know my present way of life (perhaps I am generalizing too much from my own case) is, I say, not very far removed. And these two cruel moments are, if you will forgive the expressions, which, if hardly noble, are true), these two dreadful moments are the one when you have to *fill* yourself and the one when you have to *evacuate* yourself. Two more might be added : when you learn that your patrimony is being ruined and when they admit to you the death of your faithful slaves. That, my fair saint, is my present case and it is that which I have chosen as the subject of this sad epistle.

I have felt sorry for Gothon.[4] Doubtless she had her faults, but her virtues and qualities made up for them, and there are many people in this world who have never known this compensation. Gothon loved men. But, Mademoiselle, are not men made for women and women for men? Is not that Nature's wish? Gothon, as Madame de Sade said very amusingly, '*got married because she was pregnant*'. Well, Mademoiselle, a little philosophy! Is there any great harm in it? I see nothing but virtue. It is wanting to give a father to one's child, wanting to guarantee him his food, it is wanting to raise him out of that abject class which no longer leaves misfortune any other resources than poverty and crime. . . . But she has been guilty of infidelities to her husband. . . . Well, I can find no excuse for that! Adultery on women's part is liable to such horrible inconveniences, has such sinister and fatal consequences that I have never been able to tolerate it. Examine my principles, rummage in the story of my irregularities and you will see that I have rarely disturbed this bond in my life, and that for a dozen virgins, so-called, whom I tried to seduce, you will not find three married women. So Gothon did wrong in that respect. Gothon got me arrested, I know, but death effaces all injuries in my eyes and my wretched heart can find tears even for my greatest enemies.

Despite all her faults, Gothon was attached to me. She gave pleasant, prompt, nimble service. She was a good mare and loved her master's stud. This poor wench, with the sole help of Messieurs Paulet, Payan, Sambuc[5] and company, would have provided a complete household. In truth, I miss her. Furthermore I should add – yes, now that we have been discussing virtues, we can consider physical qualities – Gothon had, it is claimed, the loveliest c—— Devil take me, how am I to explain? The dictionary lacks a synonym for this word and decency forbids me to write it in full although it is only a four-letter word. . . . Oh, well, yes, truly, Mademoiselle, it was the most fetching c—— that ever escaped from the Swiss mountains for more than a century . . . a reputation made. M. le Président de Montreuil, although matters of greater importance (which he assuredly dealt with in admirable fashion) brought him to Provence ten years ago, could never forgo any of those moments he put aside for the contemplation of that celebrated 'jewel' to which the unhappy Gothon owed her notoriety for the rest of her life. And the magistrate whom I name and who was all the more expert on that part in that his taste had been developed on the divine beauties of the Capital, was certainly well qualified to make a sound judgement on such an object. But I perceive that I am in danger of forgetting a famous proverb: 'You should never mention rope in the house of a hanged man', and that I should not therefore be occupying my mind with these immodest objects since it is claimed that my attachment to them has been responsible for all my misfortunes. But I could not deny myself this short defence, and in a good soul, whatever one's misgivings, the qualities of a person whose death you mourn crowd upon your pen as soon as your mind dwells on them and describe themselves. Let us be serious, and for the convenience of the scribbler put it on another page, for I have always been inclined to favour vice and I regard those who have the capacity to persist in them as great men. You see, we now have Jacques the scribbler[6] a 'great man'. He did not expect the compliment; no one had ever told him as much.

(The rest of the letter is missing.)

NOTES

1 A novel by Fénelon for the education of the dauphin, the Duc de Bourgogne (1699).

2 A comedy in five acts in verse (1738).

3 From Voltaire's mock-heroic poem *La Pucelle d'Orléans*. The next couplet throws light on the quotation :

> *A son époux la belle dit adieu*
> *Puis accoucha d'un bâtard qui fut Dieu.*   (*Trans.*)

4 De Sade's servant at La Coste.

5 Inhabitants of La Coste.

6 A possible allusion to Rousseau. (*Ed.*)

LETTER XII

To Marie-Dorothée de Rousset

(Vincennes, May 1782)

To Mademoiselle de Rousset wherever God has put her

Mademoiselle,

I was about to give myself the pleasure of reciprocating the honour you do me, and certainly you would have been pleased with objects which . . . all the more because . . . eh! but no, I say . . . you really would have been moved, when suddenly – as I picked up my pen, a wretched carillon[1] – the sole instrument of misfortune which I hear in this place – started up the most unholy din. As a prisoner always takes everything to himself and thinks that everything that is done is directed at him and that every remark made has him for its target – damn me if I didn't get it into my head that this wretched bell was speaking to me and saying with unmistakable clarity :

> *I pity you – I pity you*
> *But as there is no help, you must*
> *End in dust, end in dust.*

I jumped up in a frantic rage intending to knock the bell-ringer down, when to my chagrin I perceived that *the door to my vengeance* was not yet open. I then sat down again – picked up my pen, thinking I must reply to that villain in his own tongue, and in the same 'tone', since there was no alternative. And I said :

> *From joy and pleasure*
> *You needs must part,*
> *My heart, my heart.*

107

Capucin, capucin
At least he takes
A hand that shakes – that shakes.

But I have here, alas,
– this is my moan –
Only my own, my own.

Come to me then – come to me then,
And with your c——
Comfort my want, my want.

But my half, but my half
So pitiless
Makes of me a Tantalus.

Ah what fate, ah what fate,
'Tis too much ye gods on high,
I shall die, I shall die.

Sainfoin dies sans soin
Come with speed
And find the seed, the seed.

I see that I must suffer
A martyr with no peace,
Without cease, without cease.

At this point I stopped and counted. I noticed verse nine[2] ending with '*cease*' and the whole thing going to the dirge for the dead. 'Long live God! my friend,' I exclaimed, You are as witty as the Présidente; and at any rate you are as swollen as when the latter emerges from an audience with Madame Gourdan,[3] I immediately tidied up this masterpiece and I am now sending it to you so that you may see how I am keeping my brain working and how I improve my wit.

Listen, Mamselle, please send me some of our good peas of Provence – this year it has not been possible for me to eat any;

dom Sebastien de Quipuscoa has put the peas in a pudding –
ergo, I must do without them or eat those of the carriers – last
year it was cherries that were the 'signals' but he gained no
advantage because it was at my expense. He has presented a
request to Madame la Présidente to have permission to make
a 'profitable little signal' this year – oh, the rogue is no fool, I
warrant you. When one complains he replies that it is *petty* to
mention it. And so I beg you if in Provence you come across
one of those people to whom I am obliged to pay an annual
allowance and who asks for money or land, reply – fi, how
petty!

Adieu, my angel, think of me sometimes when you are between two sheets, your thighs open and your right hand busy
. . . feeling for your fleas. Remember that in that case the other
should be busy too, otherwise you have only half the pleasure.

One must be . . . like that, and the other the way Madame la
Présidente arranges her numbers.

NOTES

1 (De Sade's own note.) The church carillon. These verses must
  be sung to the tune of the carillon or thrown in the fire, for they
  are not meant to be read.
2 More allusion to the mysterious signs and signals by which de
  Sade set such store.
3 See note on p. 97.

LETTER XIII

To Madame de Sade

(Vincennes, August 1782)

Your *merits,* Madame la marquise, and your – not very witty – banter concerning my plan are not going to impress me and it is on this subject that I have the honour to reply to you at present. It is not the same with an idea as it is with a work of wit. One can easily be mistaken when oneself is the sole arbiter in a work of this kind; with an idea it is very difficult and, unless one is an idiot, impossible to fail to realize whether or not an idea is good. Now I declare to the whole universe that the idea behind my plan is a good one; have no fear that you will ever hear me boasting as much concerning one of my works. I know enough about architecture, and I have studied all the beauties of that art in Italy where my whole time was spent with men of this profession, enough to be able to decide whether or not an idea is beautiful; and, I repeat, my idea is superb and so sublime that it is impossible to put it into execution. There could be no state nor sovereign in Europe rich enough to carry it out. Thus either your designer has not said what you make out he has or else he is a fool to ask to be employed for a plan which he must feel is impossible to put into effect. It is then merely a pretty fancy – but one I cherish, and with which, one day, I mean to decorate my study. Here is a small supplement which I want you to hand him and which is necessary for the exact execution of his design. So be it!

Decidedly I shall not reply to the tedious chatter of Milli

Rousset. How can she possibly employ her mind to utter such nonsense? It is conceivable to me and I even think it moderately amusing, that someone should waste their wit on piquant subjects (that is why *Le Portier des Chartreux*[1] has never held any surprise for me) but it is inconceivable that it should be used for talk about *casseroles, rotten bedrooms, pox, kitchen utensils* and all the other stupidities the plan of which must surely have taken Madame la Présidente de Montreuil six weeks to have transcribed [*sic*] by this miserable Rousset whose genius is hundreds of miles away from it. And so her divine letter No. 223 shall be buried in the most perfect oblivion. I will debase myself to all these sordid details when I am you know where : until then I do not even want to think about the subject. Remember that I do not want a concierge paid by her : I cannot imagine how she got hold of that idea and how you could consider it for a moment. Kindly slash it down with most vigorous sword thrusts.

Of all the books you have sent me there are not two which I can read twice, and yet it is such books that I need. Fill up the enclosed catalogue; I renew my most earnest request. The *Iliad* can only be read once. The *Italian Anecdotes* are not intended to be read; they are chronological books to have on one's table when one is working, but the book no more lends itself to reading than a dictionary. I beg you to fill up my list.

Here is a little note for Amblet which I implore you to send him; and when the manuscript comes back to you, make the minor corrections contained in this note.

Since the history of the Medici family is not completed, you must not break with the doctor; on the contrary, humour him. Ah, as a friend of his, would it not have been better if they had let me shut myself up in his study in Florence to compose the said history, which would certainly have brought honour to my name one day, instead of sending me here to sort out Madame la Présidente's imbecile vomitings? . . . I propose to make a very strange wager with you and your crew : that it

will have cost one hundred thousand francs of waste expenses
for the last ten years to make me one hundred thousand times
worse than I was before and to do more than one hundred
degrees damage to the honour and reputation of my children.
Will you not admit that it is a high price to pay for the pleasure
of carrying out stupid villainies and uninspired numbers?

Formerly the doctor used to board me. A lackey and myself
at his house were fed and lodged – and very well too – for 800
livres; add another 1,200 for my keep, etc., and now calculate
what we should have gained in the last ten years. I should have
emerged from there with an additional hundred thousand
francs in my pocket, a good work to hand over to the public
and a head packed with knowledge. Look now at the other side
of the picture and see what will be the result of what you are
doing. But silence and isolation were necessary, you will say?
Ah, but that was easy, no problems : there is a French ambas-
sador in Florence who is an improvement on M. de Rougemont.
I agree that he would certainly not have played the same rôle
(it's not easy to find soldiers sufficiently debased to do it), but
Barbantane, who is no fool and is a cousin of mine would have
policed me and to discourage me from straying beyond the
confines of Florence, would have kept a *lettre de cachet* handy
which would have sent me back to the dungeon of Vincennes
within a week; he would have been responsible for my correspondence, money etc. I would go about under a foreign
name and they would tell that band of rogues who always want
me under lock and key that I was virtually a prisoner at the
Grand Duke's which they would be justified in believing since
they did not see me any more nor hear anything said about
me. That's how intelligent people behave, and how you proceed when you are utter fools and prefer the protection of
underlings to the happiness and well-being of your family.

You wanted a letter for my children? Here it is. You have
only to express a wish and I hasten to do anything you want.
My heart and my desire to please you prompt this letter – not

self-interest since I do not wish for a reply. I would a hundred times rather not write than receive very stupid and pedagogically phrased sentences back, each one poisoned with the hideous black venom of my unworthy torturer. Do not forget that I do not want a reply. They can write one if such be your wish provided it is not sent on to me.

This letter conveys my feelings about my children; it is for them, they will read it over and over and remember it. . . . Do you think now that I shall be sufficiently their enemy and my own ever to go against my principles? If I did, they would indeed despise me and justifiably. I trust this will remind you of a short 'explanatory note' I sent this winter and convince you how far I shall always be from inculcating bad principles. Oh no! such a thing would never enter into my head : if it were a choice between killing them and destroying their hearts, I should not hesitate for a moment; I would almost consider the former the lesser evil. But don't think that this is a result of my incarceration; do me at least that justice. It would have had rather the opposite effect, for I cannot think of any ill effect that my imprisonment has not had. And this is what my conviction has always been and you know it. If I may make my profession of faith here and now, you need only expect satisfaction on all matters concerning *both you and them,* I shall always strive for the happiness and perpetual comfort of all four of you. This, as you know, has been my aim at all times. That is my plan for when my troubles are finally at an end.

But as for what concerns me *personally,* I can promise you nothing. The beast is too old. Take my word for it, you must abandon his education. Julie never had any effect on M. de Wolmar, and yet he loved her well.[2] There are certain systems which are too closely bound up with life, above all when they have been imbibed with one's mother's milk, for a person to be able to give them up. It is the same with habits : when they are so enormously bound up with a person's physical make-up, ten thousand years of prison and five hundred pounds of chains would merely endow them with further strength. Perhaps I should astonish you if I were to tell you that *all such things* and the memory of them remain my refuge whenever I want to allay my present troubles. Our behaviour does not depend on ourselves, it is the result of our physique and our constitution. Our responsibility is limited to not spreading the poison and seeing that those who are around us not only do not suffer but are even unaware of our weaknesses. An impeccable conduct with our children and wife such that it becomes impossible for her – even when she compares her lot with that of other wives – to suspect her husband's bad ways, that depends on ourselves and that is what a decent man must achieve because nobody charges you with being a villain merely for an addiction to strange pleasures. Hide this addiction in public, especially from your children and never give your wife occasion to harbour any suspicion on the subject; see that your duties with her are fulfilled *in every particular*. That is the essential thing and that is what I promise. You cannot create your own virtues, nor is it any more possible to adopt anybody else's tastes in these matters than to become upright if one is born a cripple, nor to be able to adopt this or that opinion by way of moral system than to make oneself dark if one is born red-headed. This is my permanent philosophy and I shall always cleave to it. However, in 1777 I was still pretty young; the crowning misery in which I found myself might well have prepared me for my ordeal; but my soul was not yet hardened in the way you have now made it to good feeling. A somewhat different plan from the one you undertook could have achieved miracles; but such was not your intention. I thank you. I would rather confine myself to driving your 'numbers' out of my head than having to banish an infinity of little things which can charm me and appease my sorrows when I give a free rein to my imagination. You have been ill-advised; one must say that. But in all conscience, I think it is better that it turned out like this.

You must give my kind respects to Gaufridy, but I shall not

write to him any more than I shall to 'the Saint' – doubtless in the long, melancholy autumn evenings I shall think of saying some foolish things to her : apart from that, nothing.

I would like you to tell me the effects my letter produces on my children and what observations they make, but don't send any reply from them – save it for New Year's day. (P.S.) May I ask you again to get hold of the *Cabinet of Natural History*. When you fail to flatter my respectable tastes, you give me another reason for yielding to the other kind. And that is how the cursed falseness of everything that surrounds you has a double effect on me, willy-nilly, and fills my cup with evil because I lack the good fortune to discern the roads of virtue.

NOTES

1 *Le Portier des Chartreux,* by J.-Ch. Gervaise de Latouche, was published in London in 1788. (*Trans.*)

2 A reference to *La Nouvelle Héloïse.*

LETTER XIV

To Madame de Sade

(Vincennes, June 1783)

Tell me, I beg, whether it is ma' *Cordier*[1] or gaffer *Foulois-eau*[2] who objects to my having shirts. It is hospital prisoners who are refused linen, not me. How your baseness, and the low origins of yourself and your relatives are shown up by this! My dear, when I so far forgot what I *was* as to wish to betray to you what I *am*, it was perhaps to reduce you to being penni – I mean – shirtless! but not with the idea of being so myself. I hope you and your gang will remember this *mot*, until I have it set up in print.

If I wear too much linen, blame the laundress who loses for me and tears everything I possess, and then enjoin the Governor to issue orders on the subject. Not a month passes without my paying out eight or ten francs. Why should one tolerate these things!

At all events I declare to you that if I do not receive the linen I am asking for within a fortnight, I shall pack my bags, convinced that I am on the eve of my discharge. That is the only thing that can explain your stupid refusal to provide fresh linen. If there were madmen in the house one would not object to the kind of furniture in it and not be always asking for additions from one's own home. But this house is not intended for madmen : they are supposed to be put away at Charenton, not here, and the infamous meanness which causes them to be kept here should not at any rate be respected by the police at the

risk of spreading the same malady to those who do not suffer
from it. But the police tolerate everything; the only thing they
will not tolerate is insults to whores. You can be guilty of any
abuse and every possible infamy provided you show a proper
respect for whores' backsides : that is the main thing and it is
very simple – prostitutes pay and we do not. When I leave this
place I too must try and put myself to some extent under police
protection : I have an arse just as much as a whore and I should
be very glad to have it respected. I will show it to *M. Fouloiseau*
–he can kiss it if he wants, and I am very sure that *moved* by
such a prospect he will immediately inscribe my name in the
police-protected list.

They tell me that on arriving in Paris (when you had me
arrested) that was the way you set about gaining *assurance*.
First of all it was a question of knowing whether the said bottom
had been abused or not – because Madame la Présidente made
out that *I abused bottoms*. Consequently she insisted on the
visit of an expert. She is reported as saying : 'Gentlemen, look,
look, he is a little devil riddled with vices; he might well perhaps . . . how can one tell? He has so much debauchery in his
mind! . . .' And then you went off. Magistrate Le Noir put on
his spectacles, Albaret held the candle, the alguazils of Le Noir
wrote it down. And a report was drawn up as follows :

Item, having been transported to the said Hôtel de Dane-
mark, on the demand of *Marie-Magdeleine Cordier, married
name Montreuil,* we lifted the skirts of the said *Pélagie du
Chauffour,*[3] her daughter, and having carried out the inspection with due and proper care, recognized the said *du Chauffour*
as well and duly provided with two very beautiful white buttocks which were quite intact. We approached and brought up
our minions as near to the said member as we were. At their
risk and peril they parted, held open, sniffed, examined, pro-
foundly and having, like us, observed nothing that was not
healthy, we delivered the present report to serve for what is fit
and proper, anxious furthermore, as far as the aforesaid inspec-

tion is concerned, to grant the said *Pélagie du Chauffour* to be admitted to the tribunal and henceforth taken under our own powerful protection.

Signed: Jean-Baptiste Le Noir, lamplighter of Paris and born protector of the brothels in the Capital and the faubourg.

Well? Is that how it all happened? Confide in me as a friend. . . . *Furthermore* or *however it may be,* if you prefer, you haven't sent me a quarter of what I need.

First and foremost I need linen, and that urgently or I will pack my bags; four dozen meringues; two dozen large biscuits; four dozen vanilla pastilles with chocolate flavour, and not the filthy drug like you sent me before.

Whatever are those three quires of paper? I did not ask for any quires of paper : I asked you for a notebook to replace the one containing the comedy I passed out to you. Send me it and don't talk any more nonsense, for it is all very feeble. It was never made to be seized. In any case it is not going to see the light of day; when it does, the necessary corrections can be made, but I want no excisions. These things can be scored and corrected but I will not stand deletions.

Oh, my God! when will you tire of uttering so many platitudes? If you had discovered that they had had the slightest success, they would have been justified, but where have they got you these close on seven years? Admit it, you wish to harm me? To derange my mind? If so, you will all be pleased, for by God I swear that I will pay you back with interest for all your jokes : I vow that I shall grasp their spirit with a skill that will surprise you and force every one of you to admit that you've been silly idiots. I confess that for long enough I believed your Le Noir to be innocent of all these abominations, but the fact that he continues to tolerate them proves that he shares them and convinces me that he is merely a bloody numbskull like the rest.

Do not forget the night-cap, the spectacles, the six cakes of candle wax, the *Confessions* of Jean-Jacques Rousseau and the

jacket that M. de Rougemont assures me you have. I am returning a tedious novel and the 4th and 6th volume of Velly. I kiss
your bottom and I am going – else may the Devil take me – to
give myself a smack in their honour! Do not go and tell
Madame la Présidente at all events for she is a good Jansenist
who doesn't like a woman to be 'Molinized'.[4] She claims that
M. Cordier has never *forced* her except in the *vessel of pro-
pagation* and that whoever moves away from the *vessel* must
boil in Hell. And I, who was brought up by the Jesuits, I to
whom Père Sanchez taught that one must '*swim in the void*'
as little as possible, because – according to Descartes – '*nature
abhors a vacuum*', I cannot agree with ma' Cordier. But you
are a philosopher; you have another very good way of con-
ducting the matter, another narrow way and warmth in the
rectum which gives me a strong reason for agreeing with you.

I am truly yours.

As soon as you receive this letter, please call personally on
M. Grandjean, oculist in the rue Galande near Place Maubert,
and tell him to send forthwith to M. de Rougemont the drugs
and instruments which he promised to supply to the prisoner
he came and saw at Vincennes and on the same occasion you
must go and call on *your protector Le Noir* and tell him he
must see that I can take the air. And that for the sole reason
that he is able to take it all right although he is much more
guilty than I am. I have smacked a few bottoms, I agree, and
he has risked starving a million souls to death. The King is just:
let him decide between the two of us and have the guiltier one
broken on the wheel; I would agree.

Further I must have the items that have been neglected together with those requested above, a pint of eau-de-Cologne, a
head-band and half-a-pint of Orange flower water.

NOTES

1 The Présidente de Montreuil.

2 The factotum employed by the Présidente.

3 Echauffour was a property owned by the Montreuils.

4 A reference to Molinos, the Spanish theologian admired by the Jansenist sect and advocate of the doctrine of Quietism. (*Trans.*)

To Madame de Sade

(Vincennes, about 25th June 1783)

My dearest queen, there is nothing so entertaining as the insolence of your clerks. If one were not sure that your numbers[1] were riddles (concordant enough to my way of thinking), there really would be grounds for giving your clerks a good drubbing one of these days. Ah! they are going to settle my days now! What a wonderful farce it is! It rests with you, charming Princess, you who have intimate supper parties with Madame Goupille[2] (today in hospital) it rests with you, I repeat, to monopolize the hours of the Martins[3] the Albarets, the Fouloiseaus and other rogues of that kind whom you consider it right for me to regard as cab-horses made to be whipped or serve the public at any hour of any day.

Refusing to send me Jean-Jacques Rousseau's *Confessions* is yet another excellent decision, especially after having sent me Lucretius and the Dialogues of Voltaire; that shows great discernment, sound judgement on the part of your directors of conscience. Alas, they do me great honour if they believe that a deist author can be a bad book for me; I wish I could still be at that stage. You can scarcely be called sublime in your methods of cure, Father Confessors! Remember that it is the stage a person has reached that makes a thing good or bad, not the thing in itself. They cure Russian peasants of fever with arsenic; but this remedy wouldn't suit a pretty woman's stomach. That proves that everything is relative. Start from these, gentlemen, and have the good sense to realize in sending me the book I am requesting, that, whereas Rousseau can be a dangerous author for bigots of your kind, he becomes excellent for me. Jean-Jacques is for me what an *Imitation of Jesus Christ* is to you. Rousseau's religion and moral-system I find stern stuff and I read them when I am seeking edification. If you do not want me to improve, well and good! Being virtuous is hard and painful for me, and I ask for nothing better than to remain in my mire; I am happy there. You imagine, gentlemen, that your *pons asinorum* must serve everybody with the same efficacy. You are wrong and I shall prove it. There are a thousand occasions when you must tolerate one evil in order to destroy a vice. You thought you were doing something wonderful, I would wager, by reducing me to terrible abstinence with regard to *the sin of the flesh*. Well, you are mistaken. You excited me, you caused me to raise ghosts that I must now satisfy. That was passing but now it will start up again, worse than ever. When the pot boils too hard you know that it must boil over.

If I had had Monsieur No. 6[4] to cure, I should have set about it very differently, for, instead of shutting him up with savages I would have closetted him with girls; I would have provided him with so many that, devil take me, if in the seven years he has been there the oil of his lamp was not consumed! You gallop an over-fiery horse over ploughed fields; you don't shut it up in the stable. On the same principle you should have set him on the good path, what is called the path of honour. Let us have no more of these *philosophical subterfuges*, those researches that nature disowns (as if nature had anything to do with it), those *dangerous* aberrations of an over-heated imagination which, always chasing after happiness without ever finding it, end by the substitution of fancies for reality and improper deviations for honest enjoyment. . . . Monsieur No. 6, in the midst of a seraglio would have become a women's friend: he would have recognized and *felt* that nothing is finer or more important than sex and that outside sex there is no salvation. Exclusively occupied in serving ladies and satisfying their delicate desires, Monsieur No. 6. would have sacrificed his own. The habit of experiencing solely legitimate desires would have accustomed his mind to overcoming inclinations which would have prevented him from giving pleasure. All that would have resulted in leaving him appeased; and that is how I would have brought him back to the path of virtue in the very bosom of vice! For, once again, for a very vicious soul a lesser vice can be considered a virtue. *You cannot expect to get a man away from the yawning abyss in one bound;* the mere suggestion puts him off. Be content to make him form a taste for less violent pleasures, but ones that are of the same kind as those which have formed his habits. You will draw him imperceptibly away from the cesspool. But if you are too harsh and expect to take everything from him at once, you will merely aggravate him the more. You accustom a stomach to diet gradually; but you destroy it by sudden and complete fasting. It is true that there are certain people (I know some) so hemmed in by wickedness who are unlucky enough to find it so attractive, that the slightest withdrawal would put them in a state of distress; it is as if they found pleasure in their wickedness, revelled in it. For them evil is a natural state from which no effort on their part can save them : it would need a special permission from heaven and unfortunately heaven to which the good or ill of men is a matter of extreme indifference, never performs a miracle for their benefit. And the oddest thing about it is that they are not worried thereby : they would indeed be upset to be other than they are; all the anxieties, all the cares which vice brings in its train, far from becoming their torments, become their solace. It is like the harshness meted out by a belovèd mistress : one could not bear not to suffer for her sake! Yes, it is God's truth, my dear, I know such people. Oh! how dangerous they are! Let us pray to the Eternal One to preserve us from ever resembling them, and to obtain His grace, let us both repeat a *Pater-*

noster and an *Ave Maria* together with some *oremus*'s when we go to bed *in honour* of Monsieur *Saint* [name censored by a stranger hand]. (It is a signal.)

I kiss your bottom.

I beg you to recall that you sent me beef marrow in weather as hot as it is now, that I now have none at all and I beg you earnestly to send me some without fail for the fifteenth of this month. In addition a couple of night ribbons, so that I haven't always to be kept waiting later: the thickest and darkest that you can find.

Here are the exact measurements of a case I ask you to have made for me in the style of the one you sent me, but in this size – do not lessen or increase a line, and have it screwed up making sure it has a thread three inches from the top. Don't fix a ring or any ivory catches like those in the one you sent; they don't hold it. This case (for you will have to account for it to your Father Confessors) is to house plans, prints and several little landscapes I have executed in red ink. And I really believe [here one or two words have been struck out by an unknown hand] if it were for a nun, one should put [several words struck out by an unknown hand] I earnestly implore you to carry out this commission with all possible speed; all my plans and drawings are lying all round me; I do not know where to stow them.

Those who tell you that I have a good supply of linen are wrong. I possess only four wearable shirts and I haven't any handkerchiefs or towels. Send me everything I ask therefore in that line and please call a halt to your ill-placed joke on this subject. Send, send away . . . go ahead! I've plenty of time to wear it all out.

NOTES

1 Allusion to de Sade's obsession with numbers.
2 It is not known whether or not this is a nickname.
3 The Présidente's factotum.
4 A reference to his number as a prisoner. He occupied cell No. 6 at Vincennes. (*Trans.*)

LETTER XVI

To Madame la Presidente de Montreuil

(2nd September 1783)

It is not often that I importune you, Madame, and you must believe me that when I do, I must have a desperate reason for applying to you. Of all the blows you have dealt me since I have been here, none has gone home more than the one with which you have just rent my heart. You are encouraging them, Madame, to convince me that my wife is dishonouring herself. Great heavens, how can it be possible that a mother could tolerate such infamies or deliberately set out to make her son-in-law aware of them! Your scheme is terrible, but it cannot be concealed, Madame. You would have me separate from my wife and once I am out of here you do not want me to take her back. How gravely you have misjudged my feelings for her if you imagined that anything could produce such an effect. You would have me see her, dagger in hand, seeking to tear out my heart while I at her feet cry out : *'Strike, I have deserved it.'* No, Madame, there is nothing in the whole universe that can separate me from her, and I will adore her even in her vengeance. Great God, I have too much to make up for, too much. Do not make me die in despair, unable to forget all the wrongs I have committed. Love, esteem, tenderness, gratitude, respect, all the feelings which the soul can form, unite in me for her, and it is in the name of all these, and still more, I must confess Madame, in response to the cry of my conscience that I beg you to restore her to me as soon as I am out of this place.

Can you believe that so long a period of imprisonment has not forced me to reflect? Can you suppose that it has not awakened remorse? I ask you only one boon, Madame, it is to put me to the test. I do not expect you to take me at my word. I insist on being tested. Put us together and under the eyes of anyone you like and in any country where you can have me watched from morning until night for as many years as you wish, and at the slightest lapse, let them take me away and never see her again and let them deprive me for a last time of my liberty and my life, if you wish, I consent to it all. How can I express it more forcibly, Madame? Is there any better way in which I can open my heart to you? Deign to have a little pity on my state, I implore you! It is terrible. I know that this confession is a triumph for you, but I do not care. I have disturbed your peace of mind too miserably to regret providing you with triumphs at my expense. If yours consisted in seeing me in the lowest possible state of humiliation, despair and misery in which a man can find himself, enjoy it, relish it, for you have reached the goal and I wager that there is not a single being in the world whose life matters more to anyone than hers to me. Heaven is my witness that if I keep her, it is solely to try to put my life to rights and to win back the virtuous and sensitive soul of your charming daughter to whom in the terrible fever of my aberrations I have dealt such palpable blows. Oh, great God, judge of my despair and my repentance! Religion and nature equally forbid you to pursue your vengeance to the tomb; they forbid you to resist my repentance and to repel my means and wishes for atonement. To this ardent prayer, I add this, entreating you, Madame, not to secure my release from prison except to reunite me with my wife. Do not cast me into a fresh abyss of misfortune, I implore you. Do not get me out of prison only to see me return there tomorrow. For that, Madame, is what would happen, I warn you. No sooner shall I see myself free than I shall fly into her arms. Were you to bury her in the bowels of the earth, I would snatch her out and rejoin her. Once I am free, I shall rush off to M. le Noir and ask for my wife. I shall run to the minister and if he refuse me, and I am rejected on all sides, I shall throw myself at the King's feet and ask him for what Heaven has given me and men cannot wrest from me. They will thwart my steps and put me back in prison. Well, I should prefer it a thousand times to living free and without her. At least my conscience is more at peace when I am in irons; it finds reassurance in the fact that I can do nothing to satisfy it. Once free, nothing would arrest its impulses and I should either have to repair the evil I have done or lose my life. Do not therefore plunge me back into deeper misfortunes, I implore you, Madame, and get me out of here only to reunite me with her or never get me out if that reunion is not to be. Deign to allow me to see her as soon as possible and alone, I beg of you. I have some very important and private matters to discuss with her which even you must not allow others to know however much you have confided in them. Permit me, Madame, as I finish this letter – which is the last I swear I shall write to anyone however long my torture may last – permit me to throw myself at your feet to ask your forgiveness for everything that the horror of my fate has wrested from me. See only the despair of a distracted head and in that only the true feelings of my heart. I am hoping for some gesture of commiseration, Madame, I beg for it unashamed, and with you, Madame I need only blush for my wrongs.

I am with respect, Madame, your very humble and very obedient servant.

DE SADE

LETTER XVII

To Madame de Sade

(Vincennes 19th September, 1783)

This morning I received a long letter from you that went on for ever. Don't write any more of such length, I beg you; do you think that I've nothing better to do than read your wearisome repetitions? You must have plenty of time to waste, writing letters of those dimensions, and I likewise replying to them, as you will agree. But as the object of this one is highly important, please read it soberly and dispassionately.

I have just discovered three signals[1] of the greatest beauty. It is impossible for me to hide them from you. They are so sublime that I am convinced that, as you read them, you will applaud the range of my genius and the wealth of my knowledge. One might say of your *clique* what Piron said of the French Academy: *there you are, forty of you, with the intelligence of four.* It is the same with your band: there you are, six of you, with the intelligence of two. Oh well, with all your genius, and although you have been working a mere dozen years at the magnum opus, I'll lay you two to one,[2] if you like, that my three signals surpass anything you have achieved. . . . Wait, I am mistaken, there are four of them, by my faith. . . . Well, three or four and you know that the three-four combination is very powerful.

1st signal invented by me, Christophe[3] de Sade:

The first cut or tear which you will have to report to me,

you must cut off the b—— of Cadet de la Basoche (Albaret) and send them to the captive in a box. I will open the box and exclaim: 'Oh, my God, what's this?' – Jacques the prompter, who will be there, will answer: 'It's nothing, Monsieur; don't you see that it is a 19?' 'Oh, no,' I reply. . . . Without boasting, have you anything as good as that?

Second Signal by the same:

When you wish to report the *'2', the double, the duplicata, the altet ego, and pay for it twice* etc., here is how you should set about it: you must get a lovely creature to pose in my bedroom (the sex does not matter; I have a touch of your family mentality, I don't look too closely; and after all, *'mad dog*[4] . . . etc.) well, I repeat, you must have the lovely creature pose in my room in the attitude of the *Farnese Callipyge*[5] – there, presenting it attractively. I have no dislike of that part; like the Présidente, I find it more fleshy than the rest, and that, as a result, for anyone who likes flesh, it is always better than something which is shaved. . . . Making my entry, I will say to the prompter or the prompted: What is this infamy (purely for form's sake) and the prompter will reply: Monsieur, *it is a duplicata.*

Third signal, always the same:

When you want to bend backwards and make a detonation (as this summer with thunder and the lightning-conductor – a terrible effect which nearly killed me in a fit of convulsions), you must touch off the powder magazine (it is situated directly below the room where I sleep)!it will have a sublime effect.

Oh! here we have the best, don't we?

For the 4th finally:

When you want to make a 16 into a 9 (listen carefully), you must take two *death's heads* (*two,* you understand; I could have said *six,* but although I have served in the *dragoons,* I am a modest man : so I say *two*), and, while I am in the garden, you will arrange that in my room, so that I find the decoration ready when I come back. Or else you will mention some parcel sent from Provence that they have taken in for me : I will open it eagerly . . . and it will be *that* – and I shall be terribly frightened (for I am extremely nervous by nature as I have proved, on two or three occasions in my life.)

Ah, good people, good people ! take my word for it and do not invent, it isn't worth the expense of inventing things that are so banal, stupid and easy to guess. There are plenty of other things to invent and when you do not possess an inventive mind, you would do better to make shoes or enema-nozzles than invent *heavily, clumsily and stupidly.*

This 19th, and posted the 22nd

By the way, send me my linen; and tell those who *judge* that I don't need any, *judge* very badly, for Monsieur the Governor de Rougemont who *judges* very well, has just *judged* that my stove badly needs repair and has had it done. Thus, for once in a lifetime, if that is possible, let us pull the plough together, for ill-natured beasts that you are all of you, you should try not to be so to the extent of continually pulling to the right when the other is pulling to the left. Pull like Monsieur the Governor de Rougemont; he is a man of good sense, and he always pulls the correct way – or has himself pulled when he doesn't pull himself along. My valet commends himself to you so that Madame la Présidente does not forget, if he carried out signal properly, she had promised to have his son promoted sergeant.

NOTES

1 See the introduction concerning the theme of this letter.
2 (Note by de Sade.) Eh ! two to one; that's nice, I expect you wish you had found it.

3 His first name was Donatien-Alphonse-François. 'Christophe' is a blasphemous reference to Christ, à la Jarry.

4 'Mad dog etc' is an allusion to the proverb 'A mad dog cannot live long.'

5 De Sade has seen the Callipygian Venus (i.e. of the 'beautiful buttocks') the bronze statue in a collection in Naples. (*Trans.*)

LETTER XVIII

To Madame de Sade

(Vincennes, beginning of November 1783)

Oh my God! How right Monsieur Duclos is when he says, on page 101 of his *Confessions*,[1] *that lawyers' jokes always smack of the Law School*. By his leave I will improve on it and add that *they always smack of the antechamber and the foul antechamber at that*, for it is certain that in those of the faubourg one would hardly tolerate the imbecile platitudes which your mother invents with her 'book-keeper'. And so you are never going to tire of them and we are going to have imbecilities and lawyers to the bitter end! Very well, gorge yourself on them. Have your fill! I am mistaken in wanting to correct you in this matter and as I am guilty of injustice as the man who undertook to prove to a pig that a crème flavoured with rose-water is better than dung. But if you provide me with an example of obstinacy, at least don't blame me for mine. You stick to your principles, don't you? And I to mine. However, the great difference between us is that my systems are based on reason and yours are merely the fruit of stupidity.

My way of thinking, you say, cannot win approval. And what, does that matter to me? The man who adopts a way of thinking for other people is mad indeed! My way of thinking is the fruit of my reflections; it is part and parcel of my life, my constitution. I have no power to change it; nor would I if I had. This way of thought which you criticize in me is my one consolation in life; it lightens all my sufferings in prison; it com-

133

poses the sum total of my earthly pleasures and I cling to it
more than to life itself. It is not my way of thinking (but that of
other people) that has brought about my downfall. The reasonable man who despises the prejudices of the fools inevitably
becomes the enemy of the fools; he must expect it and not care
a rap. A traveller follows a good road. It has been sown with
snares. He falls into one. Do you say that the traveller is to
blame or the rogue who set the snares? If therefore, as you say,
the rejection of my principles or tastes is the price I must pay
for my liberty, we can bid each other a last farewell, for I would
sacrifice a thousand lives and a thousand liberties first, if I had
them. I take these principles and tastes to the point of fanaticism
and this fanaticism is the work of the persecutions of my tyrants.
The more they continue their vexations, the deeper they root
my principles in my head, and I declare roundly that no one
need ever mention the word liberty to me if it is offered at the
cost of their destruction. I tell you this, I will tell it to Monsieur Le Noir, I will tell it to the whole world. I would not
change even in the presence of the scaffold. If my principles
and tastes are incompatible with French laws, I do not ask to
remain in France. Elsewhere in Europe there are wise govern-
ments which do not dishonour people for their tastes nor lock
them away for their opinions. I will go and live there and
be happy.

It is not the opinions and vices of individuals that harm the
state; it is the manners of public men which alone influence
administration in general. Whether an individual believes in
God or not, whether he honours and venerates a whore or
lands her a hundred kicks in the belly, neither of these actions
will maintain or shake the constitution of a state. But if the
magistrate who should see to the supplies of a capital doubles
the price of goods because the contractors put a spell on him,
if the man in charge of public funds allows those who should
be paid from the said funds to suffer because he is misappro-
priating the interest, if the steward of a royal and numerous

household allows the wretched soldiers whom the king billets
on the place to starve to death because he wants to live like a
turkey cock, in his family (on Maundy Thursday) – then the
shock of such malpractices will be felt from one end of the
state to the other; there will be a wholesale feeling of debase-
ment and degradation. And yet the speculator triumphs whereas the other rots in a dungeon. *A state is on the brink of ruin,*
said Chancellor Olivier[2] on the bed of justice in the reign of
Henri II *when you punish only the weak, and the enriched
malefactor finds impunity in his gold.*

A king should correct the vices of the government, reform its
abuses, hang its ministers who cheat or rob him before he sets
about repressing the opinions and tastes of his subjects! I
repeat, these tastes and opinions will not shake his throne and
the indignities of those who are near it will overthrow him
sooner or later.

*Your parents, you say, my dear wife, are arranging things
with the authorities to stop me ever asking them for anything.*
This sentence is all the more singular in that it proves indisputably that one party or the other are rogues. If they think
me capable of asking them for more than your dowry it is
I who am the rogue (but I am not; roguery of that kind has
never entered my principles – it is too low a vice). If, on the
contrary, they are arranging never to give me what my children
have every right to expect, then *they* are the rogues. Make up
your mind, I beg you, for your sentence leaves no middle way.
If the latter is the case, I shall not be surprised, nor am I surprised at the difficulty they had in marrying you and at the
remark of one of your suitors : the *young lady as much as you
like, but the parents, no!* I shall no longer be surprised if they
were to pay me your dowry in i.o.u's, thereby, losing two thirds
then and there : it will no longer cause me any wonder that
people who had my interests at heart always said : *Be careful,
you do not know whom you are dealing with.* Nothing will surprise me on the part of people who contrive to avoid paying

the dowry promised to their daughter; I have long suspected that the honour of giving you three children would ruin me. This is doubtless why your mother has so often renewed her collecting of little bits of paper at my house. For the price of a few *louis* all she need do now is to have the minutes taken to the notaries and get Albaret to forge her a few notes: it is as sure as can be that I'll have to beg for alms when I leave this place. Well, what's the answer to that? There will always be three things to console me for everything : the pleasure of informing the public that has no liking for the villainies which the legal fraternity inflict on the nobility, the hope of informing the king by throwing myself at his feet, if necessary, to demand satisfaction for your parents' roguery, and if nothing comes of all that, the very agreeable satisfaction I shall have in possessing you for your own sake, my belovèd, and in using the little money that remains to me for your needs, your wishes, the sole charm of seeing you having everything from me.

NOTES

1 A reference to *Les Confessions du comte de* ***, successfully published in 1742. The book consisted mainly of portraits and a collection of anecdotes. (*Ed.*)

2 François Olivier (1493–1560) was Chancellor to François I and Henri II.

LETTER XIX

To Madame de Sade

(Vincennes, 23-24 November 1783)

Charming creature, so you want my dirty linen, my old linen? Do you realize that this is not the last word in tact? You see how much I appreciate the value of things. Listen *my angel,* I have the greatest desire to satisfy you on this point, for you know that I respect *tastes* and *whims:* however strange they may be, I find them worthy of respect both because one is not master of them and because the oddest and most singular whim of all, properly analysed, always has its origin in some principle of delicacy. I will undertake to prove it whenever you like : you know that there's no one like me for analysing things. I have then *mon petit chou,* the greatest desire to satisfy you; I would however consider myself guilty of great meanness if I did not pass on my old linen to the man who looks after me. Therefore I have done so and will continue to do so; but you can apply to him; I have already spoken to him about it diplomatically, as you may imagine. He understood me and promised to collect it for you. And so, my *lolotte,* apply to him, I beg you, and you will be satisfied. Ah, in the name of heaven! if only by so short and easy a route it were possible for me to obtain *lots of your things,* which would soon be consumed if I had them, how I would move, how I would fly! what price in gold would I not pay! Can't you hear me saying : Give me them, Monsieur, that belonged to the woman I worshipped! I shall be able to breathe the perfumes of her life; they will inflame

137

the fluid that flows in my nerves; they will bring something of her to the heart of my life, and I shall deem myself happy! Having said that, will you be kind enough, my queen, to send me some new linen, in view of my desperate need?

You ask, my little *Toutou*, in what form I want the three-hundred leafed notebook, that is six-hundred pages: well, my sweet, my reply is that I want it like the notebook I had for the *Inconstant*.[1]

O Joy of Mahomet, you say that the case I am asking for has caused you trouble. I could understand that it would if *you* had done the work, but when it was merely a question of getting someone else to do it, I cannot accept in the narrow capacity of my little brain that the simple act of ordering it, can irritate in you those impulses which convey the sensation of pain to the brain. They take you for mad, you say; this passes my comprehension; I cannot admit that the request for a *large* case by a *little* woman can cause any disorder in the pineal gland in which we atheist philosophers locate the seat of reason. You must explain that to me at your leisure, and meantime you must order the case and send it to me because I need it urgently and for lack of it, I am having to pack my drawings into something that tears them, although of the same size.

You sent me the handsome boy, *my turtle-dove, The handsome boy:* What music to my half Italian ear this word is! *Un 'bel' giovanetto, signor,* signor, they would say, if I were in Naples, and I would reply: *Si, si, signor, mandatelo lo voglio bene*[2] You have treated me like a cardinal, *my little mother* . . . but unfortunately, it is only a depiction. . . . The case then, the case at least, since you reduce me to imaginings!

Celestial pussy-cat, listen in this connection to a rather droll story which occurred in Rome during my time there. Since one must cheer oneself up sometimes: but ask Lieutenant Charles who came to cheer himself up a week ago, telling me that he was *the king's man.*

In Rome a cardinal whose name I will discreetly withhold

has a maxim that the nerve fluid set in motion every morning by the corpuscles that have escaped from the 'attractions' of a pretty wench, disposes a man's mind to study, light-heartedness and good health. Consequently a matron honoured by Monsignor concerning this interesting detail, sends a pretty young virgin every morning into the inner sanctum of his Eminence; a gentleman of the household receives, inspects and presents her. One day, signora Clementina (that was the matron's name), unaware of this ceremony and knowing that the prelate full of respect for the vestal virgin never went beyond a certain point and confined himself to habitual examinations which – in his eyes – could, if necessary, be said to be the same for both sexes, not having the daily divinity at hand, had the idea of supplying the deficiency with *a handsome boy,* dressed as a girl. Having brought the child, the signora withdrew and the gentleman carried out his inspection. 'Oh! Monsignor, what treachery!' he exclaims. 'Signora Clementina deserves to be. . . ! For a customer like you!' The cardinal approaches, puts on his spectacles, verifies the announcement, then, beaming virtuously and sending the child into his bedroom: 'Peace, peace, my friend, he says to the gentleman, we will trick *her* in her turn : *she will believe that I have made a mistake.*'[3]

This 23rd September

While we are on this subject, I will tell you then, *fresh pork of my thoughts*[4] that I have been working here trying to produce a pattern for you of the cushion needed for the infirmity of *my behind.* I was anxious for you to *test* it with your *fingers* and eyes and consequently I have cut out with the greatest skill at my command a sheet of paper on which I have traced an exact pattern of the thing; the paper is precisely as I want the cushion. You should have it stuffed with down and horse-hair (they are excellent for this) and upholstered in an ordinary stout cloth. The pattern is the exact size but it would be better to have the thing made on the large rather than the small side and it should be soft and evenly stuffed. The despatch of this cushion, *dear enamel of my eyes*, makes the thick cotton towel useless; otherwise I'll need it.

The pattern of the stockings and the small box have been sent off, *blood vessels of my heart*, and here are the carpet measurements: 42 inches long by 30 wide, of good green material with a silk ribbon binding.

Good or bad (the bad are as necessary to me as the good), I beg you, *star of Venus*, to send me all the new plays from both theatres[5] which have appeared during '83, along with the new almanacs, that is to say, at the end of next month or the beginning of January.

You can rest assured, *soul of my soul*, that the first purchase I shall make on leaving here, nay my first act of freedom after kissing both your eyes, both your nipples and both your buttocks, will be to buy forthwith: The *Meilleurs Eléments de Physique*, the *Histoire Naturelle* of M. de Buffon, quarto, with the plates, and the complete works of Montaigne, Delille, d'Arnaud,[6] St Lambert, Dorat, Voltaire, J.-J. Rousseau, with the sequel to *Le Voyageur*,[7] the histories of France and the Lower Empire, all the works which I either do not possess at all or only incompletely in my library. In view of my desire for these books and the certainty that one day I shall buy them all, look out, *mirror of beauty*, those which your funds allow you to have sent to me in the meantime, for, I do not want to borrow any more from the bookseller.

It is singularly witty, *whiplash of my nerves*, to make jokes about books, and that is where Monsieur Duclos is wrong when he says, as I reported to you the other day, that the diversions of the legal fraternity smack of the Law School: for what could be finer or nobler than to invent some conceit on a booktitle? We haven't a single writer of the century of Louis XIV or XV who ever rose to such sublimity of genius. I ask you one thing only: it is to endeavour to see that there is at least as much wit in the book as in the conceit in the title – this you have not done so far, for it is impossible to read the new novels you have sent me, although they compose the finest numbers in the world: some 59's, some 84's, some 45's, in a word, really enlightening items. Would it not be possible, *Image of divinity*, to fit all these numbers and all these long treatises in with good books? Above all in the name of God, do not buy anything of – Monsieur Rétif's[8] – He's a *Pont-Neuf* and *Bibliothèque bleue*[9] author. It is fantastic that you should consider sending me anything of his. Please send me other new and better novels.

It is absolutely impossible for me to enjoy the refutation of the *Système de la Nature*[10] if you don't send me the *Système* itself: urge that, I beg you, and tell them *'Violet of the Garden of Eden'*, that they should not oppose my welfare nor the re-establishment of *good principles*. I agree that the operation will be difficult and the principles I have adopted for thirty years, built on rock will not easily be shaken: but still you must not jeopardize the chance of success.

Seventeenth planet of space, you should not jest about hair-ribbons. First, a wife should never jest about her husband's head; secondly, *quintessence of virginity,* these ribbons are pure gratification on your part, they will never figure on any inventory, they were a free gift from you. And do you want to induce me to say, *dispenser of angelic spirits,* that this refusal is a piece of meanness? I am well aware that Lieutenant Charles over whose head one can jest, wanted to make a joke about the head-bands; but, *symbol of maidenly modesty,* now that lieutenant Charles has won his five pounds, it seems to me that you could send me hair-ribbons in the quantity and quality that you pleased. *Miracle of Nature,* I had asked you to send me a fine pair of buttocks when there was a *duplicata* to signal, but instead of that you sent me Lieutenant Charles who told me that he was the king's man! *Dove of Venus,* this is what is called taking the cause for the effect.

Rose escaped from the bosom of the Graces, it only remains for me to ask you why the refusal of the peach-wine? What analogy can there be between the constitutions of the State and the fibres of my stomach? Could one or two bottles of peach-wine, *my pet,* shake the Salic law or violate the Justinian Code? *O Favourite of Minerva* it is only to drunkards that such refusals should be made; but I who never get drunk except on your charms am never satiated, *Ambrosia of Olympus* you must not refuse me peach-wine! *Charm of my eyes,* I thank you for the fine print of Rousseau that you sent me. *Torch of my life,* when will your alabaster fingers come like that and exchange Lieutenant Charles's fetters for the roses of your breast? Adieu, I kiss it and go to sleep.

This 24th, at one o'clock
in the morning

NOTES

1 Original five-act comedy in verse by de Sade, of which the MS has never been found.

2 Yes, signor, send him, I like him.

3 The same anecdote forms the basis of de Sade's story *Attrapez-moi toujours de même* in the *Contes, historiettes et fabliaux.* (*Ed.*)

4 (Note by de Sade.) I am very fond of pork and eat very little here.

5 The Théâtre Français and the Théâtre Italien.

6 François-Thomas-Marie dé Baculard d'Arnaud (1718 – 1805), novelist and dramatist admired by de Sade and mentioned in his *Idées sur les Romans.* (*Ed.*)

7 *Le Voyageur français,* a series of 42 volumes of accounts by explorers who describe their voyages of discovery. Edited by the Abbé Joseph de la Porte, these volumes appealed greatly to de Sade. In *Aline et Valcour* he included many descriptions of hitherto unknown countries. (*Ed.*)

8 De Sade and Rétif de la Bretonne detested each other. (*Ed.*)

9 The Pont Neuf had a number of shops on it at that time, including cheap bookshops. *Bibliothèque bleue* was a series of popular books bound in blue covers. (*Trans.*)

10 Thought to refer to a book by the Abbé Bergier published in 1771 : *Examen du matérialisme ou Réfutation du Système de la Nature.* (*Ed.*)

LETTER XX

To Madame de Sade

(Vincennes, end of November 1783)

God be praised, here is the letter *with the three questions,* upon my word it took nine long months to appear and I was getting very impatient. I must have my box according to the model and no different and as soon as possible – all the books I asked you for have been published and it is pure teasing on your part not to send me them, and indeed it is very stupid and tedious of you to play your jokes about books. Of all the blunders your mentors have made it is doubtless the most extravagant.

With regard to the box, I completely fail to understand your reiterations on the point, all tradesmen make cases according to specifications and to order one for the measurements sent implies at most generosity but when you call it madness – not a word, refer rather to your cousin Villette.

You must explain to your tradesman that it is a box for stowing away arses, 'tails' – tailpieces I should say – and other little drawings which I have amused myself doing in red ink and that's why I want it. So send it I beg you because without it I am obliged to use something else which ruins, tears and crumples my arse, 'tails' – tailpieces – which is all very unsatisfactory. It is out of *modesty* on my part and not to frighten you that I was content to order a circumference of $8\frac{1}{2}$, for, at a pinch it should be 9, the measure I took from my tailpieces. But, I said to myself, nine, that's going to frighten those folk what take fright at everything; so I must settle for $8\frac{1}{2}$.

How do you expect me to be able to enjoy the refutation of the *'sistem of nature'*,[1] [*sic*] if you don't send me the book refuted at the same time as the refutation; it's like wanting me to judge a case without seeing the papers of the contending parties. You must realize that it is impossible although the 'sistem' is really and incontestably the basis of my philosophy and I am an adherent *to the point of 'martirdom'* [*sic*] if necessary, it is however impossible, seeing that I haven't set eyes on it for seven years, for me to remember it well enough to appreciate the refutation; I will do my best to capitulate if I am wrong, but at least provide me with the means. Ask Villette to lend me the book just for a week and no foolishness please, for that is what it would be to refuse me a book which I induced the Pope to read, a golden book in a word, a book which should be in every library and every head, a book which saps and destroys for ever the most dangerous and odious of notions, one that has caused most blood to be spilt on this earth and which the whole universe ought to join together to overthrow and utterly destroy if the individuals who compose this universe had the faintest idea of their happiness and peace of mind. For me, I confess myself unable to conceive that there can be people who still cleave to it, and I am utterly convinced that it cannot be in good faith. Either they are fools, people who cannot apply their understanding to anything or who do not wish or are unable to take the trouble to think things out. For it is absolutely certain that theism cannot stand up to a moment's examination, and people cannot have ever studied the most trivial operation of Nature without recognizing that nature acts alone and without any primary cause, and that this first cause which explains nothing is merely the *nec plus ultra* of ignorance.

Well, here is a letter which will doubtless *prolong* my detention, don't you agree? You should however mention to these 'prolongers' that their prolongation will be a sheer waste of time, for even if they leave me here – ten years, they will not release me in any way improved, believe me – either let them kill me or accept me for what I am, for devil take me if I will ever reform – as I have told you before, the beast is too old – there's no more hope – the most honest, sincere and sensitive of men, the most sympathetic, the kindest; I worship my children for whose welfare I would cast myself into the flames, taking to its logical extreme the scruple of neither wishing to corrupt their manners nor spoil their mind, nor make them in any way adopt my 'sistems'; I adore my parents – my own, of course – the friends that I have left and above all my wife whose happiness is my sole aim and for whose sake I have the supreme desire to make up for my many youthful vagaries – because in truth *one's wife is not made for that,* it is a truth that I have felt and expressed to her more than six months before coming in here; she will agree. Such are my virtues – as for my vices – haughty temper – easily carried away, suffering from a disordered imagination concerning morality hitherto quite unparallelled, an atheist to the point of fanaticism, that in few words is how I am, so once again, either kill me or take me as I am, for I shall not change.

NOTE
1 Work by Baron d'Holbach, 1770.

LETTER XXI

To the stupid villains who torment me

(Vincennes, 1783)

Vile minions of the tunny-fish vendors of Aix, low and infamous servants of torturers, invent then for my torment tortures from which at least some good may result. What is the effect of the inaction in which your spiritual purblindness keeps me except to curse and lacerate the unworthy procuress who so meanly contrived to sell me to you? Since I can neither read nor write any longer, this is the hundred and eleventh torture which I am inventing for her. This morning as I suffered I saw her, the strumpet, I saw her flayed alive, dragged over thistles and then thrown into a barrel of vinegar. And I said to her:

Execrable creature that is for selling your son-in-law to the torturers!

Take that, you procuress, for hiring out your two daughters!

Take that for having ruined and dishonoured your son-in-law!

Take that for making him hate the children for whose sake supposedly you sacrifice him!

Take that for having wrecked the best years of his life when it rested with you alone to help him after his sentence!

Take that for having preferred the vile and detestable off-spring of your daughter to him!

Take that for all the wickedness with which you over-whelmed him for thirteen years, to make him pay for your stupidities!

And I increased her tortures and insulted her in her pain and forgot mine.

My pen falls from my hand. I must suffer. Adieu, torturers, I must curse you.

LETTER XXII

To Madame de Sade

(Vincennes, 1783)

As acts of kindness are as deeply engraved on my heart at least as those of spitefulness, I was of course grateful for the concern shown, when the malady in my eye became apparent, in allowing the man who serves me – as in my early days here – to remain with me for a moment while I eat my meals. But in granting me this, they forgot one essential thing – *to set a limit on the items I may mention and those which I may not.* Since the mediocrity of my genius prevented me from realizing these limits, it was essential to convey to me a code relative to this subject. In vain do I wrack my brains to discover the dullest and most trivial things to discuss, I am always unfortunate enough to land myself with snubs which, as you will readily believe, would be somewhat costly but for the oath I have taken to leave to others the responsibility for my revenge. But at any rate take it they must. On two separate occasions I thought they would devour me alive – the first was for having asked *the names of the Dauphin's godfathers,* the second for enquiring *whether the surgeon would have many people to dine on the day of the fête.* So you will gather that you need to send me a small catalogue of the things I can mention lest once again I run the risk of blurting out such serious items!

Here is the crux of the matter : in the first place they have given me, as I have always said, a very insolent attendant; the thick, sour blood of this low fellow becomes sourer and more

149

heated for two reasons: first, his obligation to stay, that is to carry out a decent and human duty – two cruel conditions for a man of this kind; the second, the cause of his despair is neither more nor less than the simplicity, the indifference or banality of my conversation. I provide nothing for *the reports;* I provide no opportunties for the informer; they can't suck me dry, as they say. This makes him furious and as he is unable to vent his insolence on serious matters, he takes it out on my troubles; none of which is hardly calculated to make my life any easier. Furthermore, please tell me what this fellow means by his perpetual remark: *'Are you trying to worm secrets out of me?'* I fail to understand it, because I could not be further from doing so, secondly because it seems to me very clumsy and gauche on his part to say to me: *'Are you trying to worm secrets out of me?'* Apparently he must suffer from worms since he is afraid one should extract them from him! And there he is suddenly admitting by the stupidity of his remark two things which I did not suspect, that there's something going on behind the scenes and that he possesses the open-sesame to it all. You can see whether the people you employ are cunning or not! But this is exactly how they are. In doing so much to degrade ourselves, your mother and I, she by consigning me to a gaoler and I in becoming the butt of a gaoler's gibes, she ought at least – if there was a spark of feeling left in her earthy soul – to have these insults carried out by respectable people who, even as they distributed them, could have recommended politeness, decency and respectability in which, for the sake of her honour and mine, such infamy should be cloaked. But this boorish treatment is handed on to this man, himself extremely coarse, only by a still rougher rogue; and as these 'kindnesses' are arranged between these two comic villains to the accompaniment of loud outbursts of laughter, as no doubt they should be, and it all becomes a kind of game between them, you can judge how this behaviour is rewarded and what kind of a creature it is who is odious and infamous enough to have brought someone who is so close to her to such a pass! I rarely mention all these trivialities and when I do it is with regret, but since no one is present when this man is up to his games and he can sell you anything he wants, it is only right that I should tell you from time to time how things are going, so that you can at least judge whether they are going as you wish.

For example, today, I have had my mattresses re-made and they have stolen a quarter of a pound of wool from me. Is that a signal? If so, give the fellow a tip, for not only has he done it very well, but has gone so far as to assure me that *they shouldn't have re-made the mattress at all or that that is how they should be*. What an immortal charming piece of logic! With these people either I must do without the item requested, or I have to pay highly for it and it's very bad; there's no middle way. Those whom they used to call *brigands* in France did not hold the wretched peasant to ransom with more impunity, nor did they submit him to a relentless logic. One can say it: there could hardly be a more perfect resemblance; and yet this is a so-called 'place of corrective detention'! It is in the midst of the coarsest and lowest vices that a wretched man must learn to cherish virtue! And it is failure to respect a whore's backside that a paterfamilias has to risk losing his children's affection for ever because he is kept separated from them, that he is torn out of his wife's arms and away from the estates he administers, that he is robbed, ruined, dishonoured, wrecked, that he is prevented from introducing his children into society and from ever appearing there again himself, that he is the butt and plaything of a host of gaolers, the feeding-ground of three or four other villains and that he has to waste his time and money, ruin his health, and that for the last seven years he has been shut up in a cage like a madman! All that and why? What causes could produce such extravagant results? Did he betray the State? Did he plot to cut short his wife's days, his children's, his sovereign's? Not at all; not a whisper of such a thing. He has been unlucky enough to feel convinced that no one could be less respectable than a whore and that the way they are used should be like the way one passes a motion. Assuredly there are wrongs involved, grave wrongs which deserve to ruin a man.

If one were to go to the King of Achem, who is attended by seven hundred hussies to whom three or four hundred lashes are administered daily for the slightest lapse, and who tries out the sword on their heads, or to the Emperor of Golconda who never goes out riding except on twelve women arranged to form an elephant and who sacrifices a dozen of them with his own hand every time a prince of the blood dies, if I were to go and say to these gentlemen that there is a little corner of ground in Europe where a certain *'homme noir'*[1] daily pays three thousand scoundrels to find out how the citizens of the said little corner (people who describe themselves as *very free*) spill their spermatic matter; and that there are dungeons all ready, scaffolds erected for those of these 'very free' people who have not yet managed to learn that it was a crime to open the 'sluice', to the right rather than the left; and that the slightest excitement in the brain at such a moment when Nature urges them to open it, and the *'homme noir'* to keep it closed, was punished by death or twelve to fifteen years' imprisonment; if, I say, someone went and announced this news to the monarchs I have just mentioned, you must agree that they in their turn would have every right to shut the orator away as a madman. . . . But then these people are not policed, they have not the good fortune to be enlightened by the torch of Christianity, they are slaves whereas we on the contrary are *very Christian, very policed and very free*.

O manufacturer of this evil little round ball, you who perhaps with one single breath set ten thousand million spheres like our own in the immensity of space, you whom the death of these ten thousand million would not cost even a sigh, what amusement you must find in all the imbecilities of the little ants with which it has pleased you to scatter your globes; how you must laugh at the King of Achem who whips seven hundred women and the Emperor of Golconda who uses them as a post-chaise and the *'homme noir'* who expects one to keep one's head when one spills one's sp——! Good night, my little wife.

NOTE

1 The reference is of course to Monsieur Le Noir.

LETTER XXIII

To Madame de Sade

(Bastille, 8th March 1784)

Thirty-four months after an express refusal of a transfer to a fortress at the very door of my estates where every liberty was offered me, after a petition to end my days in peace where I was, wicked though I might be, all the time it pleased your mother to sacrifice me to her revenge, thirty-four months, I repeat, after this event, to see myself now forcibly removed unexpectedly and without warning, with all this mystery, all this comic incognito, all this enthusiasm, all this zeal scarcely pardonable in the excitement of the most important affair and after twelve years of misfortunes, as banal as it is ridiculous! And to see myself transferred to a prison in which I am worse off and a thousand times more constricted than in the wretched place where I was before! Such actions, Madame, with whatever odious lies you attempt to palliate their atrocious blackness, such actions, you must confess, deserve the culmination of all the hatred I have sworn against your infamous family. And I think that you would be the first to despise me if the acts of vengeance did not one day rival all the ferocious repetitions of theirs. But keep calm and rest assured that neither you nor the public will have anything to reproach me with on that score. But I shall have neither the virtue nor the perseverance to invent or search out in a *cold rage* whatever can render more bitter the venom which I ought to use. Everything will rise up from within me; I shall give my heart a chance, allow it free

154

play in the sure knowledge that the serpents it will produce will be at least as poisonous as those which are hurled against me.

But let us pass on to the details. It is deeds not words that are required in this case, and while one's arms are tied, one must keep silent. These are the lessons in treachery that they have taught me; I will profit by them, yes, profit, and one day I will be as deceitful as you.

For twenty years, Madame, you have known that it is absolutely impossible for me to tolerate a room with a stove, and yet it is (thanks to the attentions of those who have concerned themselves with my transference) in a room of that kind that I am now shut up. I have been so incommoded these days that I have stopped lighting fires, and that whatever the weather, I shall continue not to light any. Luckily summer is here; but if I am to be here next winter, I implore you to see that I have a room with a fireplace.

You know that exercise is more important to me than food. And yet here I am in a room half the size of the one I had before. I haven't room to swing a cat and I can leave it only rarely to go into a narrow yard where you can only breathe guard-room and cookhouse air and into which I am marched at the point of the bayonet as if I had attempted to dethrone Louis XVI! Oh, how they make one despise great things when they endow little things with such importance!

The turns of dizziness to which I am subject, the frequent attacks of nose-bleedings which I suffer when I lie down without a very high support for my head, have forced me, as you know, to have a very large pillow. When I wanted to bring away the wretched pillow, you would think I was trying to steal the list of conspirators against the State; they snatched it out of my hands, protesting that acts of such consequence had never been tolerated. And in point of fact I saw that some secret decree of the government required a prisoner to sleep with his head low, for when, as a substitute for this pillow of which they deprived me I humbly requested four miserable planks of wood, they took me for a madman. A host of officials descended on me and having verified that I was very badly bedded, gave the judgement that it was not the custom for one to be otherwise. I protest to you in truth that these things must be seen to be believed, and that if they told us that they happened in China, our soft-hearted and sympathetic French would immediately cry out : 'Oh, the savages!'

Furthermore they claim that I must make my bed and sweep out my room; the first, I don't mind, because they did it very badly and it amuses me to do it. But as for that second, unfortunately I cannot manage it at all; my parents must be to blame for not having included that particular skill in my education. The fact is there were many things they did not foresee ... many things. If they had, there would have been no tavern wench who could have rivalled me. Meanwhile I beg you to persuade the authorities to give me some lessons. Let the man who looks after me sweep it out but once a week for four or five years; I will *study* him closely and you will see that afterwards I shall manage as well as he.

For seven years I have enjoyed the use of knives and scissors at Vincennes without causing any inconvenience. I haven't improved the last seven years, of that I am well aware, but neither have I deteriorated. Could you not make that point so as to persuade them to allow me the complete use of those two objects?

I am naked, thank God, and soon I shall be as I was when I emerged from my mother's womb : I was not allowed to bring anything with me; a shirt, a night-cap caused the guard to swear and Rougemont to shout himself hoarse. So I have abandoned everything, and I beg you to bring with you without fail on your first visit – two shirts, two handkerchiefs, six towels, three pairs of list-shoes, four pairs of cotton stockings, two cotton night-caps, two head-bands, a black taffeta cap, two muslin cravats, a dressing-gown, four small pieces of cloth five square inches which I need for bathing my eyes, and some

of the books that are on my previous list. All this on condition
that I receive my boxes and other possessions from Vincennes
inside a fortnight, for, if I had to go any longer without receiving them, all those items would have to be duplicated or trip-
licated, because of the time you anticipated that I should still
be without my luggage.

Add to those things, I beg you, the following objects which
bear no relation to the trunks, that is to say I am in constant
need of them whether I receive my clothes soon or late. (Press-
ing items : my tail-cushion which I left at Vincennes, my fur-
lined slippers, my two mattresses and my pillow).

Half a dozen pots of preserves; half a dozen pounds of
candles; some packets of small ones of fifteen to the packet; a
pint of eau-de-Cologne of better quality than the last which
was no use at all; a pint of rose-water for my eyes, into which
you have first put one sixth part of brandy, that is to say five
parts of rose-water to one of brandy to the pint; and the rest
of the books which I long ago requested together with what
was left of the new comedies to fill the catalogue I sent.

Let me have the objects requested in this letter if that is
possible so that I may at least say that, for once, you have been
useful for something during my detention, and above all the
two mattresses for my bed and my large pillow. I leave the
rest to our friend in charge.

If the oculists tell you that sea-water and the powder in
question is still necessary for my eye, which is still in the same
wretched state, get them to send me these objects left at Vincennes.

Expedite the despatch of my luggage, I beg you.

Ah well! my very dear, very amiable and above all very
ingenuous wife, were you carrying out a pretty deception on
me when on each of your visits you promised that it would be
you who would come to collect me, that I should come out a
free man and see my children! Is it possible to be more basely

deceitful and false. And now tell me if you believe that those who authorize you to deceive your husband so foully work for the happiness of your life? . . . My dear wife, if they tell you that, they are deceiving you : tell them that it is I who assure you of it.

Since my return to Vincennes after all the previous horrors which I at any rate have not forgotten, since this return there remained but two dagger thrusts that you and your people could inflict : change my prison and pack my son off to a corps in which I am absolutely opposed to his serving, and without my seeing him. Both these blows you have delivered. I shall not be ungrateful, this I swear on what I hold most sacred in the world.

I send my humble greetings, Madame, and implore you to pay some attention to my letter, my requests and commissions, all the more since part of my new plan of life here is to send you nothing but lists, by which token here is my first and last letter.

[In the right-hand margin]

(P.S.)   I think you would do well to reward the guard officer for services on which I can only congratulate myself and all the more because I am now so cruelly aware of the present difference. I commend him to you.

LETTER XXIV

To Madame de Sade

(Bastille, 4th September 1784)

Madame la Présidente Cordier's sublime reasoning

For six months now my son-in-law has been irritated only in trifling matters : they have put out one of his eyes, lied to him, allowed him to take the air only on rare occasions. All that is nothing; I cannot enjoy life, my belly distends, my digestion is ruined, I have terrible nights. Torturers! approach and torture my son-in-law a little more effectively, I beg you.

THE TORTURER,
OR EX-LIFE-GUARD DE LOSME[1] :

But, Madame, he behaves like an angel. What the devil do you expect we should do to him?

MADAME CORDIER.

Scoundrel! Am I paying you to sing his praises? What does it matter to me whether he behaves well or badly! If you cannot reprimand him for his misdemeanours, punish him for his virtues. Have you no skill for creating scenes, and laying traps? Isn't that what I pay you for? My son-in-law has nobility in his feelings; insult him; he will tell you to go and f—— yourself : and you have him confined to his room and hence no more exercise. And then the idea of 'having nobility', with me who am nothing less than *noble* myself! My son-in-law is orderly in his affairs; he hates throwing his money out of the window. Make him pay 28 *livres*, 17 *sous* for an article worth only six. You can divide the profit. He will protest, he will say that he is made to pay too much for the things he buys: from then on 'buying forbidden' in order to teach him not to be a spendthrift. Thus, you can see clearly, imbecile, that if you cannot castigate him for his vices, you can punish him for his virtues! And I shall sleep again and shit in peace, etc.

To Madame de Sade

And there you have your execrable mother's infamous reasoning! And that is how this abominable extortioner leads me a dance in every way. And you expect me not to take my revenge? And you imagine that the word 'free' will cause me to forget everything? Count me the most cowardly and unworthy of men if that should happen.

At the present season air and fruit are the two sustainers of my life: between having my throat cut and being deprived of them I see not the slightest difference. We are abominably fed here. As long as I had enough to supplement this deficiency, I said nothing. But when I can no longer keep alive, I am obliged to complain. Although I might as well speak to a stone about my needs, I implore you to realize that I cannot exist without those two things and to let them choose some other way of tormenting me, if that is possible, because such torments should not affect one's needs and these two items are real necessities as far as I am concerned. If you were to see the stinking foul garbage they serve here, you would not fail to understand the need that any one who is accustomed to refined food has to supplement the diet from his own pocket. It is no longer possible to put forward the excuse of the *alleged complaint that they were robbing me,* since I have signed a certificate to the contrary. Thus it can only be spite and ill humour on your part to deny me the privilege of making purchases, and especially when you pay up as punctiliously as I hope you do. Meantime, kindly make out a list as follows:

List of the commissions which may be detached from the letter, but which I beg my wife to send me immediately.

A basket of fruit containing :

peaches	12
nectarines	12
butter pears	12
bunches of grapes . . .	12

half of everything, ripe; the unripe to be ready for eating in three or four days' time.

Two jars of preserve;

A dozen Palais-Royal cakes—six of which to be flavoured with orange-flower water—and two pounds of sugar;

Three packets of night-lights.

I beg her to expedite her despatches; and so that she may not have the excuse of insufficient money, here enclosed is an order.

I beg Monsieur the Président de Montreuil to be good enough to pay Madame de Sade his daughter without fail the sum of two hundred *livres* against the dowry arrears which I will credit to her at her first demand. Written in Paris the fourth September seventeen hundred and eighty-four.

DE SADE

NOTE
1 One of the administrators of La Bastille from 1782.

F

LETTER XXV

To Gaufridy[1]

(Paris, 12th April 1790)

I left Charenton, to which I had been transferred from the Bastille, on Good Friday. Better the day, better the deed! Yes, my dear lawyer, that was the day when I regained my liberty. So I have made a vow to celebrate it for the rest of my life, and instead of indulging in the usual concerts, aimless strolls which present-day custom condones with scant respect to religion when we should be weeping and wailing, instead, I say, of sharing in such mundane vanities, every time the forty-fifth day in Lent brings round a Good Friday, I shall fall on my knees, pray and thank God . . . resolve to mend my ways and keep my word about it.

But to the point, my dear lawyer, for I see that you, like everybody else will say: 'It's deeds we want, Monsieur, not words,' to the point then. It is established that I was landed in the middle of Paris with only one *louis* in my pocket, not knowing where to go, where to lodge, where to dine, where to get hold of any money. Monsieur de Milly, public attorney at the Châtelet,[2] who has been managing my affairs from that country for the last twenty-six years was kind enough to offer to set me up with a bed, his table and six *louis*. On the fourth day with my six *louis*, of which I had only three left, to avoid being a burden, I had to find an inn, a servant, a tailor, an eating-house keeper, etc., and all that on three *louis*.

Faced with this I presented a petition to Madame la Présidente de Montreuil, who has been good enough to promise to lend me a few *louis* through her notary, on condition that I would write to you at once to the effect that you should convey some money to me to replace the sum she has loaned me through her notary and to enable me to continue to live. And so, I beseech you, my dear lawyer, to suffer no delay in sending me the *original* sum which I asked you for the other day and my need for which is so urgent that a prompt despatch is essential.

NOTES

1 De Sade's steward of his estates in Provence.
2 Seat of criminal jurisdiction, demolished 1802.

LETTER XXVI

To Gaufridy

(Paris, beginning of May 1790)

I have just received this moment your letter of the 14th and as I see that it cannot yet be a reply to mine, I am in no way surprised not to find in it one of those charming notes which are so much more value than a love-letter and which enable one to obtain money without delay.

You must not doubt that if I did not write to you during my imprisonment it was because they deprived me of the means. I cannot forgive you for attributing my silence to any other reason. I would not have interfered in my affairs – what purpose could it have served me in my present situation? But I would have asked you for the latest news about yourself, I would have given you mine; from time to time we would have scattered flowers on the chains with which I was covered. This was not allowed. A letter which I had ventured to write on those lines was rudely returned to me. I did not write again. I repeat, my dear lawyer, I cannot forgive you for having had doubts about my feelings for you. We have known each other since childhood, as you remember; it was my friendship for you which won you my confidence; it was because of that friendship alone that I asked you to take charge of my affairs; what motive could have induced me to change my mind! It was not your fault that I was taken at La Coste but my own; I was over-confident about my safety and failed to realize with what abominable family I was concerned. I flatter myself that you will have no difficulty in understanding that I am referring now only to the Montreuils; you cannot conceive the *infernal* and *cannibalistic* designs those people have had on me. Even if I had been the lowest individual on earth they would hardly have ventured on the barbarous treatment of which I was made the victim; in a word, I have lost my sight, my lungs have been ruined and through lack of exercise I have become so monstrously corpulent that I can hardly stir; I have lost all my feelings in the process; I have no longer any taste or love for anything; the world which I was mad enough to miss so much seems stale and dismal! . . . There are times when I feel inclined to retreat to the Trappist monastery, and I cannot guarantee that I will not disappear one fine day without anyone knowing what has become of me. Never have I been so misanthropic as since I have returned among men again, and if I seem a stranger to them when I show myself in their company, they can rest assured that they have the same effect on me. I was kept very busy during my imprisonment; just think, my dear advocate, that I had fifteen volumes ready for the printer; when I left I had only a quarter of the said manuscripts. Madame de Sade, with inexcusable carelessness has lost some, allowed others to be seized, and so that's thirteen years' work gone to waste! Three-quarters of these works had remained in my cell in the Bastille; on 4th July they transferred me to Charenton; on the 14th the Bastille was taken, and demolished, and my manuscripts, six hundred books, two thousand *livres'* worth of furniture, valuable portraits – everything was destroyed, burnt, carried off, pillaged and it is impossible for me to find a single fragment left. And all because of Madame de Sade's pure negligence. She had had ten days in which to collect up my effects; she could be in no doubt that the Bastille which they had been stuffing with weapons, powder and soldiers (during those ten days) was being prepared either for *attack* or *defence*. In that case, why did she not hasten to remove my effects? . . . my manuscripts for whose loss I shed tears of blood! . . . Beds, table, chairs and drawers can be replaced but not ideas. . . . No, my friend, no, I shall never be able to convey to you my despair over this loss, it is an irreparable one for me. Since that time the sensitive and touchy Madame de Sade has refused to see me. Another woman might have remarked : 'He is unhappy, and I must comfort him'; her feelings are governed by no such logic. I have not lost enough, she wants to ruin me, she is trying to divorce me. By this inconceivable process she intends to justify all the slanders vomited against me; she is set on bringing shame and misfortune upon myself and her children so that she may live or *delightfully vegetate,* according to her, in a convent where some father confessor doubtless consoles her, smooths in her eyes the path of crime, horror and infamy on to which her conduct is to lead us all. Were this woman to receive advice from my most mortal enemy it could not be worse or more dangerous.

You will readily understand, my dear advocate, that because of sums of money formerly drawn from my wife's dowry (one hundred and sixty thousand *livres*) and for which my estate must be a guarantee, this separation will ruin me; and that is precisely what those monsters want. Alas, great heavens! I had cherished the idea that seventeen years in foul dungeons might expiate some youthful imprudences. You see, my friend, that I am mistaken. The rage of Spaniards is never assuaged. Hence Voltaire has said in *Alzire* : 'You seem to be Spanish . . . and yet you know how to forgive?'

LETTER XXVII

To Reinaud[1]

(Paris, 19th May 1790)

Yes, Monsieur, I have had the honour to tell you in the past that the best thing to do when you have the misfortune to be surrounded by rogues is to get away from them. What I set up as a maxim then I have just recently translated into action; and I thank you very much from the bottom of my heart both for the interest you appear to take in it and the marks you bestow on me of a friendship which you have been kind enough to keep for me.

Certainly the police officers of Valence were no better than the officers in the Bastille and the monks of Charenton, and once I had parted from the ones without too much fuss, I was able to take leave of the others without much ado. But I wonder if you know this story? It is piquant enough to be worth telling you.

A week before the siege of the Bastille, foreseeing clearly all the business that was afoot and that the Montreuils were not over-worried that I might like my friends gain my freedom, on the day of the siege, took the precaution of having me transferred to Charenton. There, Monsieur, those rogues, those blackguards of Montreuils whom I despise like the filth in the streets, were despicable enough to allow me to vegetate for nine months in the middle of a hospital for madmen and epileptics. . . . I am still unable to understand how it is I did not die there! . . . Finally, nine months later, my children came to visit me; one

167

of them took it into his head to ask the Prior one day by what right and authority he detained me. The latter, not daring to quote the King's orders which no one knew at that time, blamed the family. . . . 'Oh,' I then remarked to this gaoler, 'these orders are much more severe today than those issued by the ministry; I refuse to recognize them! . . . I summon you to open the gate.' The comic fellow dare not gainsay me; the two wings of the gate opened, I wished him good evening.

That is I think in accordance with the saying : the best of friends must part.

To the point now, Monsieur, in response to the friendship which you are kind enough to show me. Nothing could be worse than the shameful treatment that I am receiving at the hands of the Montreuils. They stop at nothing. Enraged to see me at large, they invent anything to awaken feelings of disgust in me when I am in the company of others. If they see me settled or anchored anywhere, they immediately send their emissaries to utter foul slanders against me. They have forced my wife to leave me. She had no wish to do so; there is nothing they have not thought up, they have left no stone unturned to force her to take this step. They were unscrupulous enough to pay journalists to tear me to pieces in their pages. In short, since I have known these monsters, would you like me to tell you what I now believe? I am more than convinced that it is they who brought up the Marseilles affair, they who bribed the girls to make them testify to horrors which had never entered my head. Ah, do not go and suppose that what I am telling you is so fanciful! A host of people vouch for it today and that my enemies not knowing how to set about separating me from the sister of my wife with whom I was living at the time, as you well know, invented this shameful way of bringing it about. . . . But enough, for my temper rises so inordinately when I speak of these f—— villains that I could only pen it with gall !

Essential business to wind up here and the fear of being hanged in Provence on democratic gallows will detain me here until next Spring. At this period, that is to say in the early days of March, I am hoping to go to Provence with my children. Those are my plans, Monsieur, which I shall carry out provided God and the enemies of the nobility allow me to live. By the way, do not take me for a madman. I protest that I am merely being impartial, angry over losing a great deal, still more angry to see my sovereign in irons, baffled that you gentlemen in Provence do not feel that it is impossible that good should be done and continue when the monarch's authority is constrained by thirty thousand idlers under arms with twenty cannon; but in point of fact regretting the *ancien régime* very little; assuredly it made me too miserable for me to lament it. Well, there is my profession of faith for you and I make it without fear.

You ask me for news; the most important today is the refusal given to the King by the Assembly to allow him any say in questions of war and peace. Furthermore, it is the provinces which provide us with everything that touches us most nearly : Valence, Montauban, Marseilles are theatres of horror where savages act out horrific melodamas in the English style which make one's hair stand on end. . . . Ah! it is long since I said to myself that this fine and gentle nation which ate the Marshal d'Ancre's buttocks from a grill only awaited the opportunity to be galvanized and show that, always situated half-way between cruelty and fanaticism, it would return to her natural tone as soon as the occasion demanded it.

But enough of that; one must be prudent in one's letters and never did despotism open as many letters as liberty.

I will end without compliments, if you do not mind. It is a remnant of our centuries of slavery which liberty should banish; please do the same, I beg you; the only way of winding up with friends is to assure them that one loves them and if you have no objection it shall be my heart that undertakes this compliment with you.

DE SADE

NOTE
1 The Marquis de Sade's lawyer at Aix.

LETTER XXVIII

To Gaufridy

(Paris, end of May 1790)

A considerable time ago I noticed a certain attitude on the part of Madame de Sade whenever she visited me at the Bastille which caused me anxiety and distress. My dependence on her made me hide it up but everything about her alarmed me. For behind it all I could clearly discern a Father Confessor's promptings, and to speak the truth, I saw with no less clarity that my liberty was to mean a period of separation.

On 4th July, on the occasion of a slight commotion that I caused at the Bastille to do with unsatisfactory treatment there, the governor complained to the minister. They accused me of rousing the mob through my window, of collecting them together under the said window, of warning them of the preparations that were being made at the Bastille, of exhorting them to raze that monument of horror to the ground. It was all true. They had me transferred to the monastery of the Friars of the Charity at Charenton, where those villainous Montreuils had the cruelty to let me languish for nine months among madmen and epileptics for whom the establishment was founded. Slightly more liberty there than elsewhere however gave me the opportunity of discovering that I was being detained only because of the monks' avarice, and that I only needed to state imperiously enough that I wanted to leave and they would fling open the gates. This is what my children and I did. I won my liberty and that well before the sanction of the King con-

cerning *lettres de cachet*, as I reported in my letter to Monsieur
Perrotet to which I refer you on the subject. But, to continue.
What is more humiliating for a man who is in his native town
with his wife and his wife's people about him than to see himself transferred from a prison where he is decently kept to one
which is altogether indecent and, furthermore, without anyone
having been apprised of the fact? You must admit that such
an action shows either evil intent or carelessness. But that is not
the whole story. When I left the Bastille on the night of 3rd
July, in accordance with the ancient customs of ministerial
despotism, I was not allowed to bring anything away. I left
therefore as naked as the back of my hand, and all my effects,
that is to say furniture, clothes or linen amounting to more than
a hundred *louis* in value, six hundred books, some of which
were extremely valuable, and what is irreparable, *fifteen
volumes of my works in manuscript* all ready to hand to the
printer, all these effects, I say, were put under seal by the officer
of the Bastille, but Madame de Sade *dined, went to the closet,
confessed and fell asleep.* Finally, on 14th July in the morning
she imagined the time had come to have the seal broken and
have my effects sent . . . to me who was still naked (luckily it
was warm weather) and still vegetating among the madmen.
Unfortunately the day she chose to wake out of her lethargy
was the same as that on which the people advanced on the
Bastille in a mob, assassinated the governor and all the officers,
which meant that all entry was barred and all my effects were
looted. I ask you, my dear lawyer, whether such behaviour is
not atrocious and whether Madame de Sade who had ten days
to herself can be forgiven for allowing me to be robbed of my
things including the manuscripts for which I mourn every day
in tears of blood . . . works which might have brought me a
good deal . . . which had comforted me in my retreat and which
soothing my solitude, had caused me to say . . . 'At least I shall
not have wasted my time!' Forgive me, my dear and valued
friend, if I pass over this circumstance; it rends my heart so

cruelly that the best thing that I can do is to try and forget
this misfortune and refrain from mentioning it to anyone.
However, I have retrieved something in the places where my
papers were thrown; nothing important, not a single work of
any consequence. Oh. 'I give it up! Great God! It is the
worst misfortune that heaven could reserve for me . . . and do
you know what the good and sensitive Madame de Sade did
to pour balm on the wound? She too who possessed many of
my works . . . manuscripts smuggled out during her visits; she
refused me them . . . she feared, she said, that these works (too
uncompromisingly penned) might do me harm in the period
of the Revolution, she entrusted them to people who have burnt
part of them! . . . My blood boils when I hear these replies! . . .
But as I am the less powerful partner, I must be content
and hold my tongue. The celestial lady of whom I have the
honour to speak to you has not restricted her kindnesses, my
dear advocate. Hardly had she heard of my release than she
made me sign a deed of separation . . . and it is this famous
document that I would like you to read. All the infamies that
have been uttered against me in taverns, barracks, compiled in
almanacs, in dull newspapers, form the basis of this wonderful
memorandum; the most unspeakable indecencies are scandal-
ously invented . . . slanderously reported. It is in a word a
monument of horrors, lies and blunders as crude and obscure
as they are flatly and stupidly compiled. And has no one parried
the blow, you say? Not a soul, my dear advocate! Three or
four counsellors have met to advise me to forget this monument
of impudence and not reply to it. I have followed their advice.
You must send me word as to whether I have done well or ill.
I will be condemned by default, legally separated, but not, I
trust, ruined. They cannot touch my possessions. Doubtless we
shall have to meet the sums of money deducted from the dowry,
but I hope that it will not prevent me having enough to live on,
and, thanks to your solicitude, my affairs in Provence can continue to remain in such a state that I shall not need to beg for

alms. You see, my dear advocate, why I am impelled more than ever to turn over to you the conduct of these wretched affairs. But enough on this subject; nothing is settled or concluded yet; let us wait. To complete the picture of my present situation and hand you at least a few roses after so many thorns, I will tell you that I am lodged with a charming lady[1] who also has been unhappy and is able to sympathize with others who have had a similar experience. She is a woman of wit and talent and separated from her husband as I am from my wife. She overwhelms me with kindness; sometimes I go along to seek distraction on her country estate, and I venture to say that, although no other feeling than that of friendship ever enters our relationship, I am never in her company without forgetting my misfortunes. It is to her that you must send my letters. She is the wife of a president of the Parlement of Grenoble and she is forty years old. I add this circumstance to allow you to see that with me who am fifty – which adds up to a good ninety between us – there is no risk involved. Furthermore I am receiving very great kindness from my own relations. Madame the Countess of Saumane, the first maid of honour of Madame Elisabeth, the King's sister; and Monsieur et Madame the Countess of Clermont Tonnerre (the latter's name is famous in the Assembly) overwhelm me with kindnesses and attention. I have found a few acquaintances and a few female friends. I receive polite attentions from them and cultivate them, all this from the centre of peace, tranquillity and the most stoical philosophy. . . . No more impure pleasures, my dear advocate, no more strange practices, that all now disgusts me as much as it consumed me before. I realize that it is all largely a matter of constitution. My physical strength hardly stands up to all the illnesses which afflict me. These include coughs, eye strain and headaches, rheumatism and in fact heaven knows what else; it exhausts me and never leaves me time, thank God, to think of anything else and I am four times happier for it. At the house of the lady of whom I have just spoken to you I occupy a little apartment at one hundred crowns a year; I can hardly turn round in it, but I feel respectably and pleasantly at home; good view, good company. I shall wait here patiently for the spring when I shall certainly come and see you and bring along my two children. You will find my children extremely gentle and intelligent but cold. I do not see them entering a poor man's house as I do at La Coste and asking about his talents, his resources and his family, and so they will never win affection. I note the fact with sorrow; but they have more than a touch of the Montreuil pride, and I would prefer to discern a little more of the de Sade energy in them. The chevalier knows Provence remarkably well. He has talked a great deal about you. Oh, you are right, my dear advocate, when you say that the sovereign blessing is living independently of other people. Nevertheless company is necessary; I felt this during my long retreat and now that my misanthropy is leaving me a little, I feel the need to spread myself. The despair of never having been able to communicate my ideas for twelve years has resulted in such a quantity collected up in my head that I must 'give birth', and I still find myself talking to myself sometimes when no one is there. I have a real need to talk; I was aware of this and because of it I see that the Trappist establishment would no longer suit me too well. By the way, we have the Trappists on the stage at the present time. After providing cardinals for *Charles IX*, nuns for the comedy of *Le Couvent* we are now having the *Comte de Comminges*, Monsieur d'Arnaud's drama, which is set in the Trappist convent. All the parts are taken by monks, the sole décor is a cemetery with its headstones. One chokes with horror, so English have we become . . . nay, anthropopaghi! . . . cannibals!

NOTE

1 Madame Quesnet.

LETTER XXIX

To the President of the Constitution Club at La Coste

(Paris, 19th April 1792)

Monsieur le Président,

If I had not just written a long letter to Messieurs your Municipal councillors, expressing the feelings which, for so many reasons, bind me to the Revolution and the French constitution, I would believe myself obliged to repeat them to you in this letter after the conclusion which I am assured has been recently made in your Assembly relative to the demolition of the crenelations of my castle at La Coste. But as I have no desire to bore you with the repetitions of phrases from my letter with which I expect you are acquainted, I will limit myself merely to begging you in this present one not to set the provinces the example of a contradiction which they would find too difficult to understand; for you will agree, Monsieur le Président, that it would seem very curious indeed to see – by the feeble light of three chandeliers – my poor house at La Coste both sullied by the unworthy minions of ministerial despotism and degraded by the enemies of the said minions; the result of which would be that, no longer knowing what decision to make or what region to inhabit, the man who must have most reasons for hating and detesting the former government, would yet find himself obliged to regret its passing, since it would become impossible for him to find defenders and friends even among those who should share his sentiments. Do you believe, Monsieur le Président, that my case would not win sympathy? Do you believe that they would not accuse those who had treated me thus of injustice? And do you believe that they would not weary me with the enthusiasm with which both in my speeches and my writings I support the Revolution to which I believe I owe much more than it is causing me to forfeit.

If they remove a single stone from the house that I own within your city walls, I will present myself before our legislators, I will appear before your Jacobin comrades in Paris and request that they engrave these words upon it: 'Stone of the house of the one who caused those of the Bastille to fall and which the friends of the Constitution wrenched from the house of the most wretched of the victims of the tyranny of kings. Passers-by inscribe this outrage in the annals of human blunders!'

Ah! leave my old hovels, Monsieur le Président! Look into my heart, open my books, read my letters printed and scattered throughout the length and breadth of Paris, at the time of the departure of the ladies of France and the flight of the King; there you will see whether the author of such writings should be the one to have his possessions interfered with. Should you be sitting on judgement on his actions? Enquire, and they will tell you whether it is not universally recognized, whether it is not authentically published that it was those crowds of people which I collected under my cell windows at the Bastille which caused me to be removed forthwith as a public danger and a man whose inflammatory behaviour was destined to raze that monument of horror. Get the minister to hand you the governor of the Bastille's letters and when you read these words: 'If Monsieur de Sade is not taken away from the Bastille tonight, I cannot answer to the King for the fortress,' you will see, Monsieur, whether I am the man to be molested. Have *I* emigrated? Have I not always gone so far as to express my loathing of such a step? Am I not an active citizen in my section? Have I not paid my guards and my taxes? Am I seen to bear any other titles than that of 'man-of-letters'? Write round my district and you will see what opinion they have of me there. . . . But

my battlements displease you! Oh well, Messieurs, calm your-
selves! It is to the whole of society that I am addressing myself;
I ask you only for the glory of sacrificing them to you myself
on the first journey I undertake in your department; the Constitution in one hand, a hammer in the other, I insist that we
make a *civic fête* of the demolition. Meantime let us make
peace, Messieurs, and *respect property*. It is from the Constitution itself that I transcribe these words; you will respect
them as I do, I am sure, and you will remember, as I wrote
yesterday to your municipal councillors, that Brutus and his
supporters had neither masons nor incendiaries when they
restored to Rome the precious liberty which tyrants were taking
from them.

I am with the most cordial fraternity, Monsieur le Président,
and gentlemen, your very humble and very obedient servant.

LOUIS SADE[1]

This 19th April 1792, rue Neuve-des-Mathurins, Chaussée de
Mirabeau, No. 20, Paris.

NOTE

1 Cf. note 3 to Letter XVII.

LETTER XXX

To Gaufridy

(Paris, 5th May 1793)

It seems to me that when one has full and unlimited power of attorney such as you have and when, by virtue of the said power, one has pledged oneself to send exactly every four months a sum of three thousand six hundred and seventy francs, and further, one of *two thousand francs* to redeem certain goods, it seems to me, then I repeat, that to come for a consultation about the means to do so is nothing more than a pretext for delay. But as, unfortunately, these delays are like a stab in the chest, since, *deprived of any letter of credit, goods to pledge and any source of loans*, I must, if you leave me to it, *literally starve to death*, then, I say, I can neither forgive nor justify you whatever these execrable delays may be that reduce me to beggary. . . . Yes, that is how it is . . . literally! For the last four days I have had no servants in the house, having no food to give them, and I myself can subsist only by dining wherever I can. In a week's time three notes of hand will fall due : four hundred francs from my lease and two hundred francs of private bills and my furniture seized if I do not pay up. It is true, my friend, yes, it is true, that on the receipt of your letter, received on the fifth day when I was without resource and when you *coldly* consult me about the means of sending me money, yes, believe me I give you my word of honour, it is true that I leapt for my pistols, and but for a friend, would have blown out my brains! . . . And you ask me, you who are on the spot,

179

you who have every power, you ask me *how you are to go about it?* ... Don't expect me to reply to this nonsense; it upset me too much yesterday for me to look at it again. In any case I cannot; they immediately burnt your letter so that, should I cast my eyes upon it again, I might not fall into the fits of rage and despair into which it had thrown me.

What I am asking of you is *money,* what I want is *money,* what I must have is *money.* I possess five hundred thousand francs' worth of property in the sun; sell without delay a plot of land to the value of the *thirteen thousand livres which I need until next May,* to avoid the cruel anxiety with which you rend my soul at every quarter. My health, ruined by prolonged misfortunes, is no longer in a state to stand up to such blows; you must stop up this hole as the money comes in, and then at any rate I shall not starve. It seems to me in the terrible suspense in which you are keeping me, that if you were to advance me my three thousand six hundred and seventy francs, you would not be taking much of a risk and you would be in a position to reimburse yourself proportionately. But such a service would be that of a friend and judging by the harrowing and cruel way in which you are behaving towards me, can I expect it?

Very well go ahead ... go ahead, in the name of God, do what you like with Saumane, Mazan, Arles, La Coste! Cut it up, nibble off it, pledge it, sell it, make a rumpus, kick up hell, but send me some money because I must have some straight away or I shall resort to the last extremity!

You are wrong to say that you cannot take anything upon yourself; your power of attorney and my confidence give you the right to take everything upon yourself ... except to keep me waiting.

LETTER XXXI

To Gaufridy

(Paris, 3rd August 1793)

The minister has received the extract from the proceedings and information relating to La Coste and they are dealing with it, but it all goes very slowly. He himself is inculpated, forced to justify himself, one has a job to see him. . . . It is true that La Coste wrote me a stupid letter; the thing that pleases me is that it is so stupid that it is impossible to reply and I am leaving it unanswered. I may tell you in this connection that the information sent to the minister is a tremendous exoneration; there is not a line which is not in their favour; a circumstance which will give the minister the embarrassment of trying to decide to whom he can now turn to satisfy my claim. I thank you for the pains you are taking in your efforts to search out the deeds which will result in my being paid what is owing to me. I realize how unrewarding, exacting and even dangerous this work is, but it is so important to me that I entreat you not to relinquish it. I get the impression that you look askance at the Bastille in the provinces. Here, it is considered a great honour to have been there; one boasts about it, publishes the fact, and it gives one a certain *prestige*. Farewell, I commend to you my three thousand and twenty francs, nine hundred and twenty of which at once and the rest on the 15th September. I am wrecked, done in, spitting blood; I told you I was Président of my section;[1] I have had so stormy a session that I am exhausted! Yesterday, as on other occasions, after being compelled to withdraw on two occasions, I had no other course than to surrender the chair to my vice-président. They were trying to make me put a monstrous, an inhuman project to the vote. I refused point blank. Thank God, I'm out of that! Adieu, think of me sometimes; I commend to you the care of my affairs more than ever and embrace you.

During my presidency I had the Montreuils put on a recommendations for mercy list. I had only to say the word and they would have had a rough time. I said nothing; that's how I take my revenge!

NOTE

1 The Section des Piques.

To Gaufridy

(Paris, 19th November 1794)

I find it hard to express the pleasure I felt, my dear citizen, on receiving your letter. I was just having dinner when I received it by a person from Avignon who assured me as he handed it to me that you were a long way from Apt and that it was very certain that, whatever pain that it might cause me, I would not hear of you for a long time. You will judge how forthright, with your letter in my hand, my reply must have been.

Well, at last you are restored to your lares and penates and I trust that you won't have to move any more. We can all feel sure, I think, that peace is about to be permanently restored. The death of the villains of the piece has dissipated every cloud and the calm we are about to enjoy will heal all our wounds.

And I too, my dear citizen, have been imprisoned. They dared to do me the injustice of believing the man whom the ministerial régime had committed to Charenton for nine months for being *suspect to the King (suspect to the nation)*. This illogicality is heart-rending for a just and sensitive spirit, but it's all over and I try to forget it. As the committee of public instruction authorized me to remain in Paris, although a noble, and that on account of my *patriotic works,* has compensated me by this favour for all the ills that those villains have made me suffer. I have been in four prisons[1] during my ten months; in the first I slept in the 'conveniences' for six weeks; in the second a week with six victims of a malignant fever, two of

whom died just near me; in the third in the midst of the
counter-revolution of Saint Lazare, an infectious poison against
which I managed to save myself only by taking incredible
precautions; my fourth was an earthly paradise; a superb
house, fine garden, choice company, amiable women, when
suddenly, the guillotine was set up literally under our very
windows and the cemetery of the guillotined right in the centre
of our garden. Within thirty-five days, my dear friend, we
buried eighteen hundred, one third of them from our unhappy
establishment. At length when my name had just appeared on
the list and I was due to be executed on the eleventh, the sword
of justice on the very eve of that day fell on the new Sylla[2] of
France. After that everything calmed down and, thanks to the
solicitude, as ardent as it was rapid, on the part of the amiable
companion who has shared my heart and my life for the last
five years, I was finally set free on the 24th of last Vendémiaire.[3]

But where the devil have you been, my dear advocate?
Your letter gives me no information as to whether your retreat
was compulsory or voluntary, and I beg you to explain it to
me when you can. Nor do you tell me who this Goupilleau is
whom you are waiting for; if he has not yet set off, I could have
seen him and spoken to him about you. My imprisonment has
now given me many friends in the Convention and I shall
always feel very flattered if I can turn this to your advantage.
My friend, animated by the same sentiments as yourself and
who also knows some of the Deputies, is likewise eager to be
helpful to you in one way or another. Just give us both our
orders. There are two Goupilleau's in the Convention, but you
don't say which one is coming to contact you. It is a tragedy
that they have sold up your harvest. Truly all these people
have behaved towards us like savages.

I congratulate you sincerely on the fact that your wife and
dear children are free. Come, take courage, everything is going
to be put to rights again and we shall no longer rehearse our
woes except to horrify our nephews.

I have learned with sorrow of the death of our friend Rein-aud. I have sincerely mourned his loss. I intend to take up the matter of the damages and interests concerning the plundering of my La Coste estates.

I think this letter is long enough for a first, but it was an opportunity to make up for lost time and above all to congratu-late each other on being in touch again. It is, I do assure you, one of the events I have regarded as the most agreeable that has happened to me for a long time, seeing that in the reign of in-justice it was very possible that only one of us might survive. Send me the list of the victims in your canton, or at least of those whom I know.

I have no news either of my aunts or my girl cousins.

NOTES

1 Les Madelonnettes, les Carmes, Saint-Lazare and Picpus.
2 Reference to Robespierre. Sylla, or Sulla, (138-78 BC), the dis-tinguished member of a Roman patrician family was likewise both ruthless and incorruptible. (*Trans.*)
3 First month of the Republican calendar (September-October).

Afterword

Sade's letters seem to me to be inseparable from any understanding of his fiction, and to provide psychological insights into this most complex and enigmatic of men which are not to be gained from reading his novels.

The very human needs of a man who like Jean Genet was a convict for much of his life, pronounce his aesthetic sensibility. Sade's requests are for meringues, orange water, vanilla pastilles with chocolate flavouring, biscuits, books, silk linen. His more practical demands are for warmth and exercise. At times he was confined to a cell in which he could not stand up, and permitted no more than thirty minutes exercise per day.

It was Sade's mother-in-law, Mme de Montreuil, who was largely responsible for his imprisonment, and Sade's realisation of this, and revolt against the hideous tortures used on convicts, make his letters not only modern, but profound in their argument against punitive measures. No thinking person today can ignore the relevance of Sade's fight against the barbarity that imprisonment entails.

Lyricism combines with humour and erotic fantasies throughout these fascinating letters. They also record the time when Sade, a prisoner in the Bastille, saw it stormed by revolutionaries. They record every facet of a great writer's response to the inner and outer worlds in which he lived.

Jeremy Reed